TO WHOM DOES THE 21ST CENTURY BELONG?

TO WHOM DOES THE 21ST CENTURY BELONG?

MANSOOR PALLOOR

ISBN:	Hardcover	978-1-4828-1391-3
	Softcover	978-1-4828-1392-0
	Ebook	978-1-4828-1390-6

To order additional copies of this book, contact
Partridge India
000 800 10062 62
www.partridgepublishing.com/india
orders.india@partridgepublishing.com

CONTENTS

PRAISE FOR TO WHOM DOES THE TWENTY-FIRST CENTURY BELONG?

After the 9/11 World Trade Center destruction, America has cleverly maneuvered the coalition of the willing to further script its doctrine of 'disproportionate response.' In it they also found a means of diverting attention from the challenges facing capitalism through pampering of corporate interests. The 9/11 attacks have been used to fashion US foreign policy along neoconservative lines, with emphasis on unilateralism, unlimited objectives, and the use of military force as a primary adjunct to policy.

It is in the backdrop of this unraveling geo-politics that Mansoor Palloor trains his sights on where our century is headed and under which key players. In *To Whom Does the Twenty-First Century Belong?* he throws into relief the arrogance of ignorance of mainly the U.S. for world-wide financial turmoil and unrest in the Arab world.

The eighteen articles, post-9/11, on diverse topics have this underlying thread of political insight. For a top executive with a Dammam-based oil company, he shows singular social commitment in addressing these grave issues.

M. P. Veerendra Kumar, chairman and managing director of Malayalam daily newspaper Mathrubhumi, author, director of Press Trust of India, member of World Association of Newspapers and Trustee Press Institute of India

No matter you are a pro-Imperialist or an anti-Imperialist, here's a book amply worth reading. The author, Mansoor Palloor, is an acclaimed columnist and writer, well-known to Malayalam readers. Given the vast spectrum of subjects of social concern he has covered in this book, it merits the attention of readers beyond the borders of Kerala. Here, Mansoor Palloor proves to be a humanist and an anti-Imperialist without being a communist. This is an out-of-the-ordinary departure from the usual practice. Most of the present-day books that deal with Imperialist atrocities perfunctorily carry the emblem of the Leftist affinities. Mansoor doesn't show such a Leftist penchant, but he is no less a mordant critic of the hurt and grief inflicted by the Imperialist regime on humanity. The thematic diversity makes the book all the more interesting. He delves into the rise and all pervading influence of the Internet and social network. His eyes that probe deep into the future hadn't missed out on the imminent economic downfall of the USA that had sent tremors all along the spine of the world. Many of the financial and political issues – that are ever disquieting – are analysed in this book sharply. Above all, what makes it a must read is the author's deep felt concern for the suffering of the people living in the redrawn geopolitical landscape of the Post Soviet Union era, from the perils of Iraq to the turmoils of the Middle-East.

M. Mukundan, one of the pioneers of modern literature in Malayalam, recipient of national and international awards including Chevalier des Arts from the French Government, Sahitya Akadami Award, and the Cross Word Award

Futurologist Alvin Toffler has competition. In this fascinating collection of writings which begin from 2001, Mansoor Palloor unplugs, predicts and demystifies the major international events since then. From someone who predicted the Wall Street crash of 2008 a year before it shook the world, here are some essays which are bound to make you revisit your views about where the world is headed.

Ramananda Sengupta, foreign and strategic affairs analyst and consultant editor, Indian Defence Review

Mansoor Palloor is a vital, incisive thinker and his new book, To Whom Does the Twenty-First Century Belong?, is an invaluable collection of his wide-ranging, systematic critique of the current crisis facing global capitalism. The 18 essays collected in the book span the period from 2001 to 2013, tracking key developments from 9/11 to the current Middle East's 'winter.' Among these are the U.S. disasters in Afghanistan and Iraq, the global oil crisis, the currency wars and the Occupy Movement. While organized chronologically, I would urge readers to jump in with 'Will Obama Turn into America'sGorbachev?' – it poses the underlying issue that unifies the book and our times.

David Rosen, culture and media critic, contributes to AlterNet, Brooklyn Rail, CounterPunch, filmmaker and Huffington Post and author of Sex Scandal America: Politics & the Ritual of Public Shaming

Mansoor Palloor is provocative. Even if you find it hard to agree with him, you cannot but help empathize. Pleased his work is being made available to an English audience.

Kannan Rajarathinam, author and political officer with UN assistance mission for Iraq

It's valuable for us in the United States to read a critique of our government's imperialism from someone outside our borders. It's extremely valuable to find such a critique drafted by an author with an informed and unflinching global and peaceful perspective. Mansoor Palloor, in his honesty and his outrage, is a true friend to the people of the United States as to the other 95% of the people of the world.

David Swanson, American peace and justice activist and author of War is a Lie

To Whom Does the Twenty-First Century Belong? is a delectable read till you turn the last page. What makes it an out of the ordinary book, uncluttered with jargon and self-serving observations, is the clinical, straight-from-the-shoulder observations that the author makes on how the West in general and America specifically attempts to spread its dreadful tentacles across the other, less privileged worlds. The author shows rare candour and conviction while answering the title of his book. He asserts that the new century does not belong to the US Capitalism. But who does it belong to, then? Mansoor cleverly leaves it to the reader to find out. Perhaps his way of encouraging the reader perception to play out.

P. P. Balachandran, New Delhi-based veteran journalist, author and columnist who worked with The Washington Post, Reuters, and Al Jazeera. His book A View from the Raisina Hill was recently released.

More and more people in the English-speaking countries are turning off the lying corporate media, and tuning in to new voices of independent global media. Among the most balanced and accurate new media voices is Mansoor Pallor, whose new book To Whom Does the Twenty-First Century Belong? captures the post-9/11 US empire in full self-destruct mode, and sketches the coming multi-polar world.

Dr. Kevin Barret, America's best-known critic of the war on terror. Member of the Scientific Panel for the Investigation of 9/11 (SPINE), author of the book 9/11 and American Empire: Christians, Jews, and Muslims Speak Out and author of Questioning the War on Terror

When reading Mansoor Palloor's thought provoking and challenging book To Whom Does the Twenty-First Century Belong? I could not help but recall the 'Project for the New American Century' the think tank concocted by a bunch of American and International NeoCons Zionists the likes of William Kristol, Robert Kagan, Paul Wolfowitz, R. James Woolsey, Elliot Abrams, John Bolton among others, whose vision of America post Cold War turned from a vision of military dominance in world affairs to disastrous and total failing military interventions in Iraq, Afghanistan costing America trillions of dollars taking America to the brink of financial and economic failings. The Project of the New Century was the start of the finish of America as a world dominating power.

Like the Soviet Union before it, America have seen better days and it's unlikely that America's economic, financial and military power will sustain it as the 'only' dominant world force.

Latin America was able through popular and daring movement to free its self of total American dominance and the world is now watching if the Arab and Muslim world will also free itself from chocking American dominance that brought the region nothing but disasters from endless wars, wasting trillions of badly needed infrastructure on military spending without ever winning any wars, depriving populations and citizenship from decent lives and a chance for a place under the sun. We must not underestimate the irreparable damage and failings done to societies thorough collusion of the military, political and established religious establishment and the pseudo presence of 'elected institutions' that were nothing but a joke, a fraud and a lie. The Twenty-First Century will belong to those who chose life over death, those who celebrate life achievements rather than 'martyrdom', those who chose knowledge rather than ignorance, and those who take matters into their hand through hard work take the 'will of God' to achieve great things and to those who must stop blaming 'colonialism and imperialism' for their own failings. Renaissance begins with emphasis on education, education and more education, knowledge through science, technology. New social, religious and cultural value systems that nurture the good things we have and add to it what we need. The book is a must read by those who can make a difference.

Sami Jamil Jadallah, BA, MPA, JD (Indiana University) is a Palestinian-American born in Palestinian city of El-Bireh (presently under Israeli Military and Settlers Occupation), a veteran of the US army, columnist and founder, executive director of New Arab Foundation, a not-for-profit 501 (c) (3) think tank

Mansoor Palloor's To Whom Does the Twenty-First Century Belong? is a collection of insightful essays that deeply study and probe into one of the most challenging and debatable concerns of our time, i.e. the

American imperialism. From a critical and investigative perspective, Mansoor deals with the perilous ideology of imperialism that has cost the lives of thousands of innocent people in the contemporary era, and underlines the plight and suffering of nations across the world that have been subject to the insatiable greed of the United States for power, energy and natural resources. Mansoor eloquently talks about the ordeal of the Iraqi, Afghan, Iranian and Venezuelan people and other independent nations that have been militarily, economically or politically attacked by the United States as the world's foremost imperial power. Mansoor Palloor's book is an honest scrutiny into what has made the United States an unfriendly and unpopular superpower for the world nations, especially in the Middle East. This book is truly worth reading several times, especially given that its author illuminates and embellishes his personal viewpoints with statistics, figures and quotations to substantiate his claims and make them reliable and trustworthy.

Kourosh Ziabari, award-winning Iranian journalist and media correspondent with Tehran Times

An amazing book! An objective eye opening must read for all those who truly care about the future and the world we're creating for our children and the generations to come.

Jonny Punish, political and eco-activist, syndicated columnist, and solo music artist. His top tracks include 'The Magnificent Afghanistan', 'The Occupation', 'We're All Human Beings', 'Peacemakers', and 'War No More'.

Mansoor Palloor's To Whom Does the Twenty-First Century Belong? is a compelling examination of the American empire and its one-sided wars over the course of 12 years.

Mansoor Palloor doesn't pull any punches as he narrates, with admirable honesty, the belligerent behavior of a hastily declining empire in a desperate attempt to clench onto its remaining global hold. As China, India and other global powers rise in influence and import, the US rapidly declines, as Mansoor demonstrates with ample authority. The wars on Afghanistan and Iraq seemed frantic attempts at ensuring that the 21st century would be an American one, to no avail.

To Whom Does the Twenty-First Century Belong? is an astute account of the gigantic shifts happening on the international scene, written with authority and with unabashed candor. Mansoor's account is also free from the confines of ideology and self-imposed limits of 'experts' analyses' and other drivels often offered by mainstream media.

It is a book that I read with great interest and I strongly and proudly recommend.

Ramzy Baroud, an author, internationally syndicated columnist, and the editor of PalestineChronicle.com

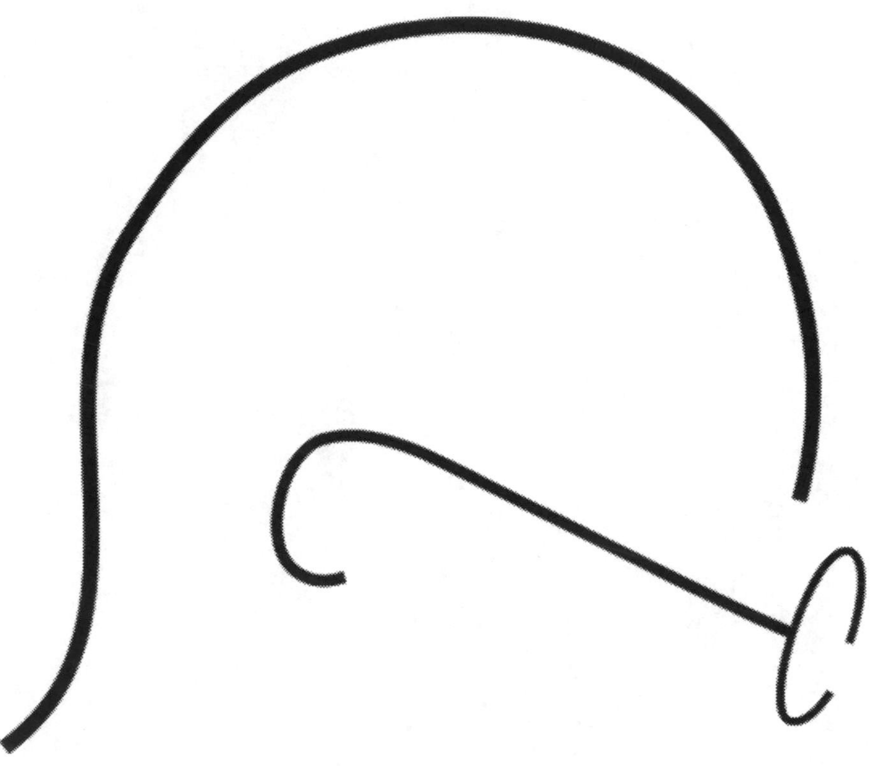

This book is dedicated to Gandhian philosophy of non-violent resistance and peace.

FOREWORD

A DEFENCE AGAINST IMPERIALIST INVASION

The print and electronic media of our time are now shrinking into a very narrow network. That is, the general public watching television and reading newspapers get to know only those pieces of information which the journalists consider important, ignoring the events of significance which affect not only us but our future generations as well. Again, under the onslaught of announcements and declarations by high-standing officials, the lives and necessities of the common man get ignored. Often, the image of these leaders is not the one created by them among the public but rather the exaggerated images projected by the media.

Often, while making news *sensational* by weaving in the controversial parts of statements by the American president, British prime minister, or the ever-shifting power centres in the form of autocrats of Pakistan, the media does not enlighten the viewership with the connotations or political significance of these statements. Hence, the audience, especially the younger generation, turns parochial or rather grows up as frogs in the well. The administrators can easily make the masses bow down to the policies encouraging imperialism by taking advantage of their ignorance.

The notion that foreign affairs are the monopoly of some specialists and those who waste their time eavesdropping on neighbouring houses, ignoring one's own, is a false one. Our major newspapers know Iraq, Afghanistan, and Palestine only as volatile regions haunted by suicide bombers.

A few writers in Kerala do possess the insight and knowledge to analyse pieces of news and their connotations, digressing from the system, embracing ignorance and a kind of suicidal apathy. Among this handful, Mansoor Palloor is a notable writer. *To Whom Does the Twenty-First Century Belong?* is a collection of his essays written and published in diverse journals and newspapers from 2001.

The first essay was written year after the dawn of the twenty-first century. Confining all the happenings of this eventful period fraught with wars, alliance formations, dissolutions, and economic crises to a handful of essays is an impossible task. Nevertheless, Mansoor has definitely succeeded in unveiling the essence underlying the eventfulness of this period.

Just as the constitution is the basis of India's all civil and criminal laws, the United Nations Charter is the basis of all international laws and policies. The charter says that the conflicts between two nations should be resolved without resorting to war through discussion between the two. If a solution is not reached thus, the decision must be left to the UN. The United Nations Charter also has the provision to make a dissenting nation accept the UN's decisions through peace talks or by force using military force from nations other than the ones involved in the issue. All this is part of the international legal code set up to ensure global peace by eradicating conflicts between nations and the consequent war-like atmosphere. Unfortunately, today, in the UN, since the countries exhibiting the highest criminal tendencies are given prominence and five nations among them have veto power to annul the majority opinion, it is impossible to put into practice the well-meaning founding principles of the UN. Hence, the world is not free of war even after the establishment of the United Nations Organisation.

As the United Nations, which had been established with the aim of ensuring global peace, completes its sixty-fifth year, it is to be noted that it has been a silent witness to numerous wars. In these sixty-five years, over hundred minor conflicts and more than fifty wars, resulting in bloodshed, have taken place. Wars like US–Korea, US–Vietnam, US–Afghanistan, US–Iraq, Israel–Palestine, India–Pakistan, Iran–Iraq, Georgia–Russia, and the Balkan Wars involving the NATO (the North Atlantic Treaty Organisation formed under the leadership of America) abounded. Besides, there were a number of civil wars in Africa, Sudan, Sri Lanka, and so on. The undeniable common factor in most of these wars is the role played by the American empire. And in the case of the minor wars in which it does not intervene directly, America sides with one or the other party and supports bloodshed. Mansoor Palloor gives voice to these facts in his unique way. His articles also impart to us a consciousness of morality and a desire for the freedom of humankind, as well as an awareness of the necessity of different cultures and economic systems to cooperate and coexist.

A notable fact about all the American imperialist wars is that America has not managed to win even a single one. America, who had to retreat humiliated from Korea and Vietnam, although it has military stations in Iraq, attack bases in Afghanistan, and a *proxy* stance in the Israel–Palestine problem, is struggling to escape from these countries. Why does the world's greatest military power have such a pathetic plight? Mansoor puts forth a number of facts regarding this and comes with insightful conclusions. The most significant of these observations is that from its first place in terms of power, America is sliding down to the second or third place. It won't be possible for those acquainted, even to a limited extent, with global events to refute the claims Mansoor makes, quoting many an American writer, that their dream of an *American century* will remain an illusion.

This plight that has befallen America is not just about military or political power. From time immemorial, it has been the economic power of nations that supported its military and political power. Mansoor proves deftly that America's financial superiority is just a farce, that it is the American dollar—serving as the means of global financial exchange—that covers up this farce, and that the dollar would soon have to give way for other currencies.

But I do not see the possibility of a new currency replacing the dollar that Mansoor talks about, any time in the near future. Today's world is a community of 192 nations, including countries with less than a population of 50,000 and countries with a population of over 100 crores. Many of these countries do not have even the capability to send ambassadors to the other 191 countries. While such gargantuan disparities exist, it is impossible, at least for the time being, to have a common currency acceptable to all. The large-scale sale of the book *One World* by Wendell Willkie, the brilliant and highly imaginative politician who competed with, and finally succumbed to, President Franklin Roosevelt during the Second World War, had attracted many a naive reader. The concepts of one military, one parliament, and one currency for the construction of *one world* were the products of Willkie's imagination. Although it is good intentioned, Wendell Willkie's imaginary paradise, just like Francis Bacon's *Atlantis*, Thomas More's *Utopia,* and Campanella's *The City of the Sun*, which were mere imaginative writings which failed to see reality as reality, was a work which gave birth to illusory dreams. I believe that Mansoor Palloor, with his deep consciousness of history, reality, and knowledge about realities, will not fall prey to such dreams. This does not mean that such a currency system will not ever come into existence. It is just that such a possibility will not rise any time in the near future. Besides, how can we be sure that there will not be a world order without currencies at all?

It was the Bretton Woods Conference of 1945 that laid the base for America's dollar dominance. Owing to the new economic conditions, the status of the dollar as the medium of transaction in the global market is slipping away. The core tenet of globalisation had been that just as all countries have the right to import goods freely, they should also have the right to export goods to other countries without such hassles as tax, and now, America is considering ways of stopping imports from other countries. The textile industry, motor industry, and computer software industry of America have been facing huge crises for the past ten years. Once they requested India to reduce the textile imports to America. They pleaded with Japan to halt the import of Toyota cars to America for some time. Following the huge financial crisis, which began last year, George Bush had also begged China to give a loan from its dollar deposit to America. They are making such requests and adjustments with several European countries as well.

As we look back, we will be surprised by the daring Mansoor who prophesied in 2007 itself that such developments would lead America to a financial crisis, not unlike the global financial crisis of 1929. In 2007, Mansoor had written with reliable statistics and extracts about the Wall Street crisis of 2008, which had shocked the American officials, capitalist theorists across the world, and crores of ordinary shareholders. It is also notable that the developments predicted by Mansoor in his article titled 'America Becomes a Pauper' published in the editorial of the newspaper *Madhyamam* became realities within the next one year.

When the UN was formed in 1945 at America's Dumbarton Oaks, there were 45 members in it. Now, the number has increased to 192. Although many of these countries are America's lapdogs, the drastic change in power relations in the world cannot be ignored. From 1945, the Soviet Union had been in the habit of annulling major resolutions which were not to their liking, using veto power. The post-war US presidents like Truman and Eisenhower alleged that the Soviet Union was insulting public opinion. But, from the 1960s, when the nations of South Africa and Asia began freeing themselves from the West through struggles and negotiations, veto power, or rather the right to insult public opinion, became America's property. Even now, many of the resolutions at the UN General Assembly are against America. And the majority often votes against the US. Added to this crisis at the global level is the military and economic breakdown of the US. Mansoor argues that this crisis has been brought about by America's military and political violence and the spiralling defence (defence, in the jargon of today's betrayal politics, means attack on other nations) expenses. That is, global peace is the only solution for the economic stability of not just one's own country but of the world as a whole.

America and its policies were guided by the belief that, with the fall of the Soviet Union and East Europe in 1990 and their return to capitalism, it would be easy to carry out its greed-induced imperialist mission of establishing a single-pole autocracy over the world. But

George Bush Sr and Bill Clinton, who were the presidents during this time, went forth, keeping their goal in view, without resorting to boasting or arrogance. It was after George Bush Jr came into power in 2001 that the imperialist attempt at 'single-pole autocracy over the world' was carried out through massacres and unilateralism (i.e., taking decisions on its own without discussing it even with friendly nations, let alone the UN). Although America is led by Barack Hussein Obama and his stances are motivated by positive goals, doubts as to whether he will be able to dismantle the imperialist policies rooted in American life, administration, and economic system are alive. Most observers believe that this will be an impossible mission for Obama to accomplish. Mansoor Palloor also seems to endorse this view.

The very history of American development is one of violence, both internal and external. While the Monroe Doctrine introduced by America in 1830 and the Philippine attacks of 1898 were external, the atrocities committed on aborigines in the United States of America were internal.

The ignorance and apathy of our media towards international issues and the perils they bring about have been discussed at the very beginning of this foreword. In such circumstances, writing such articles and publishing a book like this is the need of the hour.

—P. Govinda Pillai (Written for the Malayalam edition)

PREFACE

> To put the world right in order, we must first put the nation in order; to put the nation in order, we must first put the family in order; to put the family in order, we must first cultivate our personal life; we must first set our hearts right.
>
> (Confucius)

This book titled *To Whom Does the Twenty-First Century Belong?* is a collection of eighteen essays written by me. All the articles are on topics related to American imperialism and its impact on the Middle Eastern countries.

The American policies of intervention in the sovereignty of other nations and its self-appointed role as the apostle of global democratisation had been a part of its foreign policy since the time of Woodrow Wilson (1913-1921), the twenty-eighth president of United States America. But the notion that extending the reign of America across the world is divinely ordained; that is, manifest destiny has been in prevalence in the American political arena from the eighteenth century itself. The belief that the spreading of the boundaries of freedom as defined by America across the world is a divinely ordained mission has been inculcated in the populace of America from this period. The same feeling of being divinely entrusted with this responsibility can be seen reflected in the inaugural speeches of American presidents time and again. Herman Melville (the author of *Moby Dick*), one of the greatest American novelists, has talked about this mission in his *White Jacket* (1850):

And we Americans are the peculiar, chosen people—the Israel of our time; we bare the ark of the liberties of the world. Seventy years ago we escaped from thrall; and besides our first birth right—embracing one continent of earth—God has given to us, for a future inheritance, the broad domains of the political pagans, that shall yet come and lie down under the shade of our ark . . . God has predestinated, mankind expects great things from our race, . . . The rest of the nations must soon be in our rear. We are the pioneers of the world; the advance-guard sent on through the wilderness of untried things, to break a new path in the New World that is ours. And let us always remember that with ourselves, almost for the first time national selfishness is unbounded philanthropy; for we cannot do a good to America but we give aims to the world. (*White Jacket*, page 151)

Many of the global conflicts, as well as the imperialist desires of America, are inextricably linked to the notion of manifest destiny. The Palestine problem and the Iraq War are a few examples. It is the same inspiration that propelled George Bush Jr to declare that he had received a divine vision exhorting him to attack Iraq.

We saw the imperialist strategy of manifest destiny reaching its most dangerous phase during the reign of George Bush. I believe that through these articles, I have succeeded in reacting adequately against this and made the readers aware of the dangers inherent in the American policies rooted in this notion of manifest destiny. I have not followed the method of quoting history under the shadow of current events. The events of the past have been read side by side with the current realities, analysed, and responded to. Hence, reports and quotations substantiating my viewpoints have been used quite a lot. I remember how, when the article 'America Becomes a Pauper' was published in a Malayalam newspaper *Madhyamam* in 2007, many people dismissed it as a mere flight of fancy.

Most of the articles in this book were initially published in *Madhyamam*. I have chosen the articles related to this topic from the ones published at different times.

I express my heartfelt gratitude to my friends Naushad Anchal, Soman Pandakkal, Adv. Sajith C. T., and Girish Babu, who encouraged me to undertake this task, as well as to my friends Jacob Abraham, Chandran Kuniyil, C. Gangadharan, and V. N. Sasi who supported me in all the initial stages of publishing this in English. I am particularly thankful to Mohammed Shariff, editor of *Saudi Commerce and Economic Review*, who did the final editing of the book, and to Girish Macreri for his artistic skills in designing the book cover.

The foreword to the book containing the Malayalam versions of the first nine articles in this work was written by the late Marxist thinker and writer P. Govinda Pillai to whom I am indebted. This foreword has also been included in this book.

The world is changing. After the failure of communism, now global capitalism has also collapsed. With the downfall of Uncle Sam at his first step, the state of the New World order remains unpredictable. Let's pray that the upcoming global movements would lead to the welfare of humankind.

Mansoor Palloor

1

THE HUNTER AND THE HUNTED

It is not often that we hear about the plight of the Afghan people, who are casualties of the first war of the twenty-first century, from mainstream media. The gruesome details found in the war reports dispatched by reputed journalists from Afghanistan are not for the faint-hearted. Channels like BBC and CNN have extensively covered the visual feast that the world's mightiest hunter, the United States, has laid out before them. Unfortunately, those channels like Al Jazeera, which often reports news unpalatable to the United States, are a rarity. Various print media outlets have reacted to the war in Afghanistan in entirely different ways. Although many intellectuals within the United States were opposed to the war from the outset, their views were largely ignored by the media.

The renowned American writer Gore Vidal addresses this issue in his latest work *The End of Liberty*. Vidal vehemently criticises the United States government and national media for failing to find out the causal links behind the 9/11 terrorist attacks. Although a prestigious American magazine approached Vidal with an offer to host his column on the 9/11 attacks, the magazine refused to run his opinions when he finally sent it in for publication. The reasons for this, in hindsight, are not too difficult to seek. Vidal's criticism contained strong words of reproach against American policies, which may not have gone down well with the public.

What was his criticism, then?

Vidal wrote on the numerous attacks and unwarranted aggressions that America had carried out on other countries; sometimes, these were even covert wars on nations accused of 'harbouring Communists'. If you keep attacking nations and their citizens, they will retaliate one day, he warned. Vidal also described the American war on Afghanistan as unjustifiable. 'Osama bin Laden is not a nation, but an individual. Al-Qaeda is a gang—just like the Mafia. You don't attack Italy because the mafia is hosted in its city of Sicily. Osama could just as easily have been apprehended with the help of Interpol.'

Although it is controversial, Gore Vidal's argument that the American war in Afghanistan has a hidden agenda is not without substance. As the Afghan invasion winds down, America already has its sights set on 'rogue nations' like Libya, Sudan, and Syria. While Uncle Sam readies himself for another war, it is not easy to forget the dubious foreign policy objectives of this country, about which its own citizen-author William Blum described America as the most rogue nation in the world responsible for the killing of innocent lives across the globe; in Vietnam, Korea, Japan, Cambodia, Yugoslavia, Somalia, Haiti, Chile, Nicaragua, East Timor, Panama, altogether in around 100 countries, they conducted 400 overt military interventions and over 6,000 covert interventions. The records behind the acts of unilateral aggression show wanton killing of civilians. Since the first 'intervention' that it carried out in the Dominican Republic (1798), America has flouted all norms of international law to preserve its military interests. Only five of America's such military interventions have been declared wars as required by US Constitution!

The UN Charter, which has been ratified by all member countries of the world, forms the cornerstone of international law. According to Articles 41 and 42 of the charter, member nations have the right to initiate military action against a country that poses a threat to their peace and security but only after obtaining permission from the UN Security Council. By circumventing this requirement and acting unilaterally against Afghanistan and Iraq, Britain and America have destroyed the very fabric of UN law.

It may be worth noting that the former president of Yugoslavia, Slobodan Milosevic, is currently facing trial for violating wartime laws and killing tens of thousands of innocent civilians during Bosnian War (1992-95). Similarly, former US Presidents George Bush Sr and Bill Clinton ought to be prosecuted for killing thousands of children and innocent civilians during Iraq War in 1991. Although it is difficult to ascertain the casualties in Afghanistan at the moment, thousands of people have been killed, without doubt, owing to the merciless bombing by Western forces. Alongside Osama bin Laden, the likes of George W. Bush Jr and Tony Blair have to be brought before the law for their actions. Today, the world lives in a shadow of fear, generated by the euphoric call to war by an American president. 'Either you are with us, or you are with the terrorists,' thundered George W. Bush Jr The words reflect the sentiments of the world's largest autocracy.

Seen in this context, the reports sent by eminent journalists from Afghanistan make for a fascinating read. While heavy bombing continued overhead, against one of the most bankrupt nation in the world, British reporter Gary Johnson was offered a share of his meal—a piece of potato, a slice of onion, and a piece of nan flat bread—by a Taliban fighter, who was well under twenty. When asked through an interpreter what his reaction was to the attacks of 9/11, the puzzled youth, carrying Kalashnikov rifle, inquired what this event was all about. Johnson, a seasoned reporter, was left speechless.

For a second, I wondered what I was doing, sitting in a dust-ridden track in the middle of nowhere, far from family and friends, watching this curious battle where some of the combatants appeared to have little idea why the US military might was being wielded from the heavens.

(*The Mirror*'s Gary Jones on the Afghan friends he will never forget after eight weeks in their devastated land (3 December 2001))

Jason Burke of the *Observer News Service* has a different story to tell. We are told that the Americans have knocked out the Taliban command and control centers.

He writes, 'I have seen many of these. They largely consist of a man sitting on a rug with a radio, an ancient, unconnected telephone and the mother of all teapots.' ('Why This War Will Not Work', Jason Bruke; *Observer*, 21 October 2001)

Perhaps the lack of a desired effect from these devastating attacks on 'command and control centres' may have prompted the United States to bomb other civilian installations and food aid distribution centres in Kunduz, Kandahar, and Gardez. What followed was a terror far more deplorable than the atrocities committed on 11 September 2001 when 3,000 innocent lives perished. This is exactly the message that Robert Fisk, the Middle East correspondent for *The Independent*, sought to convey when he recounted an attack against him in an Afghan refugee camp.

And—I realised—there were all the Afghan men and boys who had attacked me who should never have done so but whose brutality was entirely the product of others, of us—of we who had armed their struggle against the Russians and ignored their pain and laughed at their civil war and then armed and paid them again for the 'War for Civilisation' just a few miles away and then bombed their homes and ripped up their families and called them 'collateral damage'.

So I thought I should write about what happened to us in this fearful, silly, bloody, tiny incident. I feared other versions would produce a different narrative, of how a British journalist was 'beaten up by a mob of Afghan refugees'.

And of course, that's the point. The people who were assaulted were the Afghans, the scars inflicted by us—by B-52s, not by them. And I'll say it again. If I was an Afghan refugee in Kila Abdullah, I would have done just what they did. I would have attacked Robert Fisk. Or any other Westerner I could find. ('My Beating by Refugees Is a Symbol of the Hatred and Fury of This Filthy War', Robert Fisk, *The Independent*, 10 December 2011)

Armed with his wry sense of humour, Robert Fisk describes how the twenty-first century has made the hunted as dangerous as the hunter. When terrorists attacked the Indian parliament in December 2001, the leader of the war on terror asked us for evidence. In the same breath, the same 'global policeman' vetoed a UN Security Council Resolution, condemning the use of uranium bombs in Palestine. Keep your eyes open for more cruel jokes.

28 December 2001

Weapons ready for launch

Plumes of smoke billow from the World Trade Centre towers in New York City after a Boeing 767 hits each tower during the 11 September attacks

2

TO WHOM DOES THE TWENTY-FIRST CENTURY BELONG?

The cries that heralded the birth of this new century have not subsided. News and stories about terror attacks and massacre of civilians have become so commonplace that they don't disturb our conscience any more. When the media is busy serving us stories of lewd acts and gossip, where is the time to think about the future of this century?

Four days after the Soviet Union had collapsed, I remember sitting with the doyen of Malayalam literature, O. V. Vijayan, in his Chanakyapuri flat during a winter in Delhi. 'Now new models of warfare will threaten our existence,' predicted O. V. Vijayan. He reminisced at length about the American export of wheat to India, which contained some genetically modified seeds that caused health problems here—eventually requiring the help of US corporate pharma companies to sort the issues. In that meeting, O. V. Vijayan had also expressed his doubts over the role of imperialist forces in the assassination of former Indian Prime Minister Rajiv Gandhi, who had been killed six months before.

The passage of time has proved many of O. V. Vijayan's assertions to be true. After the cold war, America spearheaded many acts of invasion and aggression globally. New acts and models of warfare are still being chalked out in the drawing boards of Washington. The legacy of many covert wars continues to haunt societies in different corners of the world. In India too, the Kargil War and, on a lesser scale, the funding problems faced by the Marxist party in Indian state of Kerala are all symptoms of this covert warfare. Intellectuals affiliated to the Left ideology like M. N. Vijayan blame the CIA for the troubles that the Marxist party in Kerala encountered in its early days. To know who were on the payroll of the CIA, we will now have to wait for the autobiography of CIA executives, who are currently resigning in droves.

The shameful stories of how our former Defence Minister George Fernandez, who had been a firebrand socialist in the Opposition, had prostrated before the United States were revealed through former US Deputy Secretary of State Strobe Talbott's narrations in his book *Engaging India*. Eminent journalist B. R. P. Bhaskar had already disclosed how the CIA used the help of academicians to achieve their ends in India. Several members of the US academia had toured Kerala, wearing a Marxist visage.

I was reminded of these covert tactics after reading Robert Kaplan's commentary on 'Supremacy by Stealth' in *The Atlantic*, wherein he had defended America's tools of secrecy in perpetrating the forces of globalisation. Some important aspects in his article include the following:

1. It has proved easy to manipulate professionals in the service sectors of many countries to rise up in social unrest against their regimes. Such secretive operations are vigilant and relatively cost-effective.
2. Apart from military tactics, warfare on the economic, industrial, business, and even environmental front has proved to be useful sometimes.
3. Rather than letting the media focus on one troubled flashpoint in the world, it would be easier to divert the world's attention to many corners. In such fashion, the prospects of dominating the globe become brighter.
4. Offering military aid is the easiest way to access a country's defence infrastructure. That is why the US is always ready to offer

military help to other countries; the military bases abroad also serve as control centres to dictate terms.

5. The US cannot afford to neglect any corner of the world. America's aim is not to colonise or militarily dominate; it is to gain supremacy through private or secretive ties and linkages.

Let us analyse the extent of American supremacy through the prism of 'rules and tools' that Robert Kaplan has devised. After the curtains fell on the cold war, America has focused its energy and military and economic might to subjugate other nations and subvert their independence. Consequently, it has established military bases in all parts of the world except Antarctica. The Pentagon, which forms the headquarters of America's defence establishment, calls these bases as the European Command, Pacific Command, Southern Command, and Central Command.

According to one of the reports of Pentagon, America has 725 military bases in over 138 countries across the world. In Pakistan alone, America has four military centres. Among the Gulf countries, Qatar, Bahrain, Yemen, Kuwait, and Abu Dhabi host such military facilities of the US.

Rather than boosting international ties through the adoption of cultural and strategic links, America's proclivity to dominate the world is best evidenced by a proliferation of these military bases. Schools tomorrow will likely teach their students on America's neo-imperialist schemes perpetrated by military means. It is estimated that nearly 500,000 American soldiers have been deployed in different parts of the world. Thirteen naval bases have been set up by America in high seas across the globe, named after presidents right from George Washington to Ronald Reagan. In addition, there is a vast network of intelligence apparatus that spies on people, including American citizens, to extract information as a formal Naval Officer Chamers Johnson points out in his recently published book *Sorrows of Empire.*

It was in 1992, during the presidency of George Bush Sr, that America declared itself to be the world's super cop that could intervene in any country which faced a crisis. Later, in 1997, a group of conservatives including Jeb Bush (George Bush Jr's brother and Florida Governor),

Dick Cheney, Donald Rumsfeld, and Richard Armitage came together to publish an action plan called Project for the New American Century to preserve and protect America's security, interests, and growth. The said plan favoured a change in circumstances that would bring ruling regimes across the world in line with America's interests. Many saw this controversial plan as a blueprint for American military and economic neo-imperialism.

If the public saw American neo-imperialism earlier as a figment of the Left's imagination, it has now turned to reality, much to everyone's chagrin. On 1 June 2002, George Bush Jr declared in the military academy at West Point, 'We must uncover terror cells in 60 or more countries, using every tool of finance, intelligence, and law enforcement.' Just as some Muslim-named terrorists act in the name of jihad, distorting the message of Islam, George Bush Jr has contorted the words of Christ found in the Testament. 'He who is not with me is against me' (Matt. 12: 30). This statement has been used by Bush to force nations to side with the US in the War on Terror. Bush's ideology is similar to that of Roman Emperors Cato and Cicero—'until they fear you, their hatred of you is insignificant'. Hitler began the Second World War in 1939, citing the threat posed by Poland. Bush winning his second presidential term in November is comparable to Hitler's election victory of 1933.

We've read about the collapse of the mighty Roman empire, and the fall of Hitlerism is a part of history. The twentieth century stood witness to the end of the British empire where the 'sun never sets'. The seventy years old soviet communism and Soviet Union melted like snowflakes in the sun is all but a naked truth. A few years back, we saw the first signs of American economic might swaying in troubles when frauds exposed the chinks in the armour of US monopoly companies like Enron. America's relentless wars for oil were aimed at helping it save itself from this breakdown. America, which occupies just 4 per cent of the world's total area, is using up almost 40 per cent of the world's energy sources. How long can they continue this consumerist greed through financial and military exploitation?

Francis Fukuyama was one among the think tanks who had worked behind the controversial project for the New American Century. In his *The End of History*, he had predicted that global capitalism and the single world order had heralded the 'end of history'. But the history of the not-so-far-away future would prove Fukuyama's argument wrong and show that the twenty-first century would mark the collapse of the American capitalist imperialism reigning in full splendour now.

6 December 2004

Then US President George W. Bush delivers a speech, commemorating the sixtieth anniversary of the attack on Pearl Harbour to a group of Pearl Harbour survivors and sailors of the Atlantic Fleet on the flight deck aboard USS Enterprise

O. V. Vijayan

3

IN THE OFFING—AN ALL-INCLUSIVE PLAN FOR IMPERIALISM!

The modern society has more possibilities and freedom of choice come with it than the earlier generation. Using technology, we can communicate and control machines; similarly, with the aid of technology, the entire nervous system can be controlled and manipulated. It was first brought into the world's eye by the eminent scientist Nobert Weiner (1894-1964). His book *Cybernetics* became an instant success around the world. It is quite a coincidence that George Orwell's *1984* got published in 1948 the exact same year. George Orwell's idea is that the world revolves around an epicentre of power: the big brother. Orwell predicted about such an age in technology that would scan man's each and every word, deed, and utterance with an uncanny knack, but this gave an uneasy chill down the spine for the readers of *1984*.

We cannot just set aside Orwell's idea as impractical. There are a lot of private companies that already use this type of technology to monitor the employees and their asset. These screening devices in the shape of very compact and discreet buttons are available in the market. The prediction that the world will be under the constant observation has come true.

The father of information technology, Japan's Yoneji Masuda (1905-1995), had forewarned quite early in 1980 that Orwell's kind of cybernetics technology will handcuff the freedom-loving human race. The idea to surgically insert a microchip into the human body and connect it to a satellite so as to monitor and coordinate his every move through a computer has been developed by imperialistic forces like America. The *Daily Washington Post* in May 1995 reported that one such chip has been incorporated into Prince William's (Britain) body. It was speculated that if Prince William were to be abducted, the satellite would trace the signals and thereby find them.

America is planning to insert microchips which are smaller than mustard seeds into newborns to collect important data pertaining to the personality of each individual like fingerprints. Such babies who have been incorporated microchips can be monitored; their each step can be watched. In such a case, the big brother may even introduce terrorist prevention inoculation just like disease prevention inoculation all around the world in the near future. The father of IMI biotic medicine, Dr Carl Sanders, claims that this experimental technology was done in American soldiers during Iraq War.

With the view of performing a single global government, US and Britain formed the Council on Foreign Relations. Its founding member Zbigniew Brzezinski published a book in 1970, *Between Two Ages: America's Role in the 'Technetronic Age'*. Brzezinski's book deals with a proper vigilance over all citizens and makes sure a controlled society will come in the near future. Zbigniew Brzezinski has served former US presidents Kennedy (1960), Jimmy Carter (1977-1981), and Ronald Regan as security advisor. Dr Johannes B. Koeppl, PhD, a former German defence ministry official and advisor to former NATO Secretary General Manfred Werner, has this to say about Brzezinski's book '*The Grand Chess Board*': 'It is an autocrat's blueprint to world dominance'.

American military intelligence has been experimenting sophisticated and satellite technology on human brain and its activities so as to control it. These experiments raise a significant threat to the future and existence of the human race. The infamous behaviour-modifying programme MKULTRA, funded by CIA and developed in corporation with the

Yale University's Director of Neuropsychiatry Dr Jose Delgado, tried to implant an electrode into a bull's brain and control the bull, using the radio signals.

This visual was telecast in 1985 by the CNN channel. Here is what Dr Jose Dilgdo has to say about this on that episode:

We need a program of psychosurgery for political control of our society. The purpose is physical control of the mind. Everyone who deviates from the given norm can be surgically mutilated. The individual may think that the most important reality is his own existence, but this is only his personal point of view. This lacks historical perspective. Man does not have the right to develop his own mind. This kind of liberal orientation has great appeal. We must electronically control the brain. Someday armies and generals will be controlled by electric stimulation of the brain. (Congressional Testimony of Dr Jose Dilgdo, 1974).

The word of Dr Jose Dilgdo hangs like a sword of Damocles over the future of mankind. In the future, what science and technologies demand from man is not free mind, clarity of thoughts, or ideological brilliance but strict adherence to obedience and blind belief. Fifty years ago, Orwell predicted about such a technetronic society, which is under the strict surveillance, and the big brother is already trying to do just the same.

In the coming twenty years, man will be able to amalgamate nanotechnology, biotechnology, and information technology. These three, when integrated with them the most recent scientific know-how, will throw new light into the evolutionary blueprint of man. This was sighted in a 405-page report in America's National Science Foundation. If this becomes a reality, the information could be downloaded from computer to man and communication could be done as telepathy. The army will be deployed and controlled by technological means. To overcome the erosion of ethical values due to this, a complete reorganisation of the education system is essential from the primary level, the report suggests.

If the encroachment into privacy—cultural, economical, and emotional freedom—by imperialistic superpowers becomes a reality, then it is left to you for imagining what happens next.

1 August 2004

George Orwell

Nobert Weiner

4

FALLUJAH, THE STORY THAT THE CYBER WORLD TELLS

Blogs, appearing on Internet screens worldwide, have become a sort of fifth estate over mainstream newspapers. These Web blogs are mostly written in the form of diaries or journals published daily or on intermittent days. If one wants to know the cruelty in Iraq and also the plight of the Iraqi people, you should browse the blogs, and that was the advice given to me by one of my Iraqi friends staying in Qatar. When Iraq's interim Prime Minister Ayad Allavi declared emergency in Iraq and when the US forces declared it as the beginning of the end of Iraqi liberation, we cannot forget these stories appearing in these blogs. One such blog called 'Secrets in Baghdad' written with ethical annoyance by Khalid tells the following story:

Tuesday, 9 November 2004

I am alive, I don't know about the kicking, but I know that I am definitely alive . . . am I? My heart is bleeding, my soul is burning, I die every time I see the news . . . but the stupid scientists insist that since I have heart beat, I am still 'alive'. well, I am not perfectly good biologically good either, this stupid flue is keeping me half-drunk, maybe it's better to keep it this way for now . . .

I just decided yesterday, who is the person I hate most in this world, it is definitely Allawi, I won't call him names cause I know that many young fellows read this too, but I really need to, so give me one minute, I will go curse and scream, and I will be back.

Ok, much better.

Over 75% of the families left Falluja, some people decided to stay with their families, they prefer to die on the soil of their beloved city, under the the walls of their own houses . . .

If it's true that people of Falluja asked Allawi, ok I need another minute here—ok, if it's true that they asked him, like he said, to go invade Falluja to liberate them from the Zarqawi, how come we NEVER saw ONE person out of the 75 % who left the city, on TV saying this? How come that we have never seen ONE person from Falluja saying that in real life? In newspapers? In radio? How come? how come that EVERY single person we see on TV, in real life and in the newspapers, curses Allawi, and says that there isn't any Zarqawi, at least not in Falluja? the man they set his house to the ground in Falluja, and killed his baby son, carries him on front of the camera and said: This is Azzarqawi, I am sure this is Azzarqawi, why else did they kill him? the young man who just came back from the mosque, right after the sunset prayer, which is the time to break the fasting everyday day, was supposed to find his father and mother, sisters and brothers sitting around the table, waiting for him to eat with them, but he found them dead, all of them, the house that was bombed, fell on them . . . two churches were bombed in Baghdad yesterday, while Falluja is in the middle of the battle that needs every man and every weapon, is it still possible today to accuse this city of these terrorists acts? Isn't Azzarqawi busy defending himself? while you are reading this and enjoying the silence in your houses and offices, people in

Falluja are dying and burning, screaming, 12,000 soldiers are trained and sent to kill them, for no crime except that they have pride, except that they wouldn't accept to be occupied, except that they swear to live with honor, and die with honor . . . close this window, get back to your life and enjoy it, I hope you all get nice sleep at night, and don't bother thinking of us, or pushing your administration, they are just 'bad people' and you are liberating us, long life America!

Just like Khalid, River Bend is a woman blogger who has posted the story *'Baghdad Burns'*. She is a 24 year old blogger who writes from an unknown corner in Iraq, who caught the attention of the whole world. This is what she has to say to us.

Wednesday, 10 November 2004
Rule of Iraq Assassins Must End . . .

I'm not feeling well—it's a combination of the change of weather and the decline in the situation. Eid is less than a week away but no one is feeling at all festive. We're all worried about the situation in Falloojeh and surrounding regions. We've ceased worrying about the explosions in Baghdad and are now concerned with the people who have left their homes and valuables and are living off of the charity of others.

Allawi declared a 'State of Emergency' a couple of days ago . . . A state of emergency *now*—because previous to this week, we Iraqis were living in an American made Utopia, as the world is well aware. So what does an 'Emergency State' signify for Iraqis? Basically, it means we are now *officially* more prone to being detained, raided, and just generally abused by our new Iraqi forces and American ones. Today they declared a curfew on Baghdad after 10 p.m. but it hasn't really made an impact because people have stopped leaving their houses after dark anyway.

The last few days have been tense and heart-rending. Most of us are really worried about Falloojeh. Really worried about

Falloojeh and all the innocents dying and dead in that city. There were several explosions in Baghdad these last few days and hardly any of them were covered by the press. All this chaos has somehow become uncomfortably normal. Two years ago I never would have dreamed of living like this—now this lifestyle has become the norm and I can barely remembering having lived any other way.

My cousin kept the kids home from school, which is happening quite often. One of the explosions today was so close, the house rocked with the impact and my cousin's wife paled, 'Can you imagine if the girls had been at school when that happened—I would have died.'

Dozens of civilians have died these last few days in Ramadi, Falloojeh, and Samarra. We are hearing about complete families being killed under the rain of bombs being dropped by American forces. The phone lines in those areas seem to be cut off. We've been trying to call some relatives in Ramadi for the last two days, but it's next to impossible. We keep getting that dreadful busy tone and there's just no real way of knowing what is going on in there. There is talk of the use of cluster bombs and other forbidden weaponry.

We're hearing various stories about the situation. The latest is that 36 American troops have been taken prisoner along with dozens of Iraqi troops. How do people feel about the Iraqi troops? There's a certain rage. It's difficult to sympathize with a fellow-countryman while he's killing one of his own. People generally call them 'Dogs of Occupation' here because instead of guarding our borders or securing areas, they are used to secure American forces. They drive out in front of American cars in order to clear the roads and possibly detonate some of those road mines at a decent distance from the American tanks. At the end of the day, most of them are the remnants of militias and that's the way they act. And now they are being used in Falloojeh against other Iraqis. The whole situation is making me sick and there's a fury building up. The families in Falloojeh have been relegated to living in strange homes and mosques outside of the city . . . many of them are setting up their families inside of emptied schools and municipal buildings in Samarra and neighbouring areas. Every time I see Allawi on TV talking about his regrets about 'having to attack Falloojeh' I get so angry I could scream. He's talking to the outside world, not to us. Iraqis don't buy his crap for a instant. We watch him talk and feel furious and frustrated with our new tyrant.

I was watching CNN this morning and I couldn't get the image of the hospital in Falloojeh being stormed by Iraqi and American troops out of my head—the Iraqis being made to lay face down on the ground, hands behind their backs. Young men and old men . . . and then the pictures of Abu Ghraib replay themselves in my mind. I think people would rather die than be taken prisoner by the Americans.

The borders with Syria and Jordan are also closed and many of the highways leading to the borders have been blocked. There are rumours that there are currently 100 cars ready to detonate in Mosul, being driven by suicide bombers looking for American convoys. So what happens when Mosul turns into another Falloojeh? Will they also bomb it to the ground? I heard a report where they mentioned that Zarqawi 'had probably escaped from Falloojeh' . . . so where is he now? Mosul?

Meanwhile, Rumsfeld is making his asinine remarks again,

'There aren't going to be large numbers of civilians killed and certainly not by U.S. forces'.

No—there are only an 'estimated' 100,000 civilians in Falloojeh (and these are American estimations). So far, boys and men between the ages of 16 and 60 aren't being counted as 'civilians' in Falloojeh. They are being rounded up and taken away. And, *of course* the US forces aren't going to be doing the killing: The bombs being dropped on Falloojeh don't contain explosives, depleted uranium or anything harmful—they contain laughing gas—that would, of course, explain Rumsfeld's idiotic optimism about not killing civilians in Falloojeh. Also, being a 'civilian' is a relative thing in a country occupied by Americans. You're only a civilian if you're on their side. If you translate for them, or serve them food in the Green Zone, or wipe their floors—you're an innocent civilian. Everyone else is an insurgent, unless they can get a job as a 'civilian'.

So this is how Bush kicks off his second term. More bloodshed.

'Innocent civilians in that city have all the guidance they need as to how they can avoid getting into trouble.'

How do they do that Rumsfeld? While tons of explosives are being dropped upon your neighbourhood, how do you do that? Do you Stay inside the house and try to avoid the thousands of shards of glass that shoot out at you from shattering windows? Or do you hide under a table and hope that it's sturdy enough to keep the ceiling from crushing you? Or do you flee your house and pray to God you don't come face to face with an Apache or tank or that you aren't in the line of fire of a sniper? How do you avoid the cluster bombs and all the other horror being dealt out to the people of Falloojeh?

There are a couple of things I agree with. The first is the following:

'Over time you'll find that the process of tipping will take place, that more and more of the Iraqis will be angry about the fact that their innocent people are being killed . . .'

He's right. It is going to have a decisive effect on Iraqi opinion—but just not the way he thinks. There was a time when pro-occupation Iraqis were able to say, 'Let's give them a chance . . .' That time is over. Whenever someone says that lately, at best, they get a lot of nasty looks . . . often its worse. A fight breaks out and a lot of yelling ensues . . . how can one condone occupation? How can one condone genocide? What about the mass graves of Falloojeh? Leaving Islam aside, how does one agree to allow the murder of fellow-Iraqis by the strongest military in the world?

The second thing Rumsfeld said made me think he was reading my mind:

'Rule of Iraq assassins must end . . .' I couldn't agree more: Get out Americans.

Friday, 12 November 2004

One of Those Weeks . . .

These last few days have been explosive—literally.

The sounds seem to be coming from everywhere. I've gotten tired of running upstairs and out on to the roof to find out where it's coming from. It feels like the first days of the war sometimes—planes, explosions, bullets, smoke . . . roads cut off.

We haven't attempted to leave the house but an uncle who was supposed to visit called to say he wouldn't be able to come because so many roads were blocked. Many people were told not to go to work and students stopped going to college yesterday. It's one of those weeks. Some areas in Baghdad seem to be cut off by armed gangs.

Eid is in a couple of days and that means there's Eid cleaning to do. The water was cut off all day today and the electricity was gone too. This seems to be happening all over Baghdad—we heard about the same situation in several areas. Can someone say 'collective punishment'?! WE didn't kidnap your relatives Allawi . . . it was Zarqawi, remember?!

Falloojah is still being destroyed and the stories we hear are mixed. It's difficult to tell what's true and what isn't. All we know is that there are dozens of civilians being killed. They also say 18 Americans have died and over a hundred are wounded.

Mosul is also a mess. They are saying there isn't a tank or patrol car in sight in that city.

Read more about the situation at Juan Cole—would love to say more but the generator is going to be turned off in a couple of minutes.

The blogs from Iraq are refreshingly tinted with truth, and these blogs provide with flesh and blood account of the atmosphere in Iraq that is otherwise missing in the current media reports available for our perusal. During the first Gulf War, the world was glued to CNN effect, whereas during Afghan War, it was the Al Jazeera effect. During Iraq War, it was blogs from Salam Pax that created media frenzy in the world.

For the one and half years of war news of Iraq, when the news of Chemical Ali being killed in an airstrike was rumoured, the main news for the millions of bloggers in front of the computer screen was Salam Pax, who disappeared all of a sudden. Some technical issues had crept up. That was the reason for the abrupt disappearance of Salam Pax, it was told.

For its dispassionate and detached description of events from the Iraqi war front, 'Baghdad blogger' Salam Pax became a cult figure. Salam's fame spread far and wide, and it brought Britain's *The Guardian* to Iraq. After systematic research, *The Guardian* found out the man behind Salam Pax—a twenty-nine–year-old architect. Salam now writes columns for *The Guardian* too.

For the newscaster worldwide, the situation in Iraq has lost its novelty. They have diverted all their attention to Yasser Arafat. It was during this time that America intensified the missile and bomb attacks in Fallujah. The official death tolls alone divulge the fact that more than 1,500 Iraqis were killed as an aftermath of the atrocities in Fallujah. On Monday, 8 November 2004, America began its second phase of attacks in Fallujah. The first American military operation of Fallujah in April was an utter failure. So they have come better prepared with a vast army this time. The American rationale behind the attack of Fallujah is the presence of Al-Qaeda's Iraqi leader Zarqawi, a Jordanian. If we take into account the data from some reliable agencies about the 2700 attacks and conspiracies against American occupancy in Iraq, Zarqawi has instigated only a meagre eight of them.

The famous journalist John Pilger quotes some lines from the Shura Council's 14 October letter to Kofi Annan:

> In Fallujah, [the Americans] have created a new vague target: al-Zarqawi. Almost a year has elapsed since they created this new pretext, and whenever they destroy houses, mosques, restaurants, and kill children and women, they said: 'We have launched a successful operation against al-Zarqawi.' The people of Fallujah assure you that this person, if he exists, is not in Fallujah, and we have no links to any groups supporting such inhuman behaviour. We appeal to you to urge the UN [to prevent] the new massacre which the Americans and the puppet

government are planning to start soon in Fallujah, as well as many parts of the country. (Iraq: The Unthinkable Is Becoming Normal, *The Independent*; 20 April 2003). John Pilger says not a word of this was reported in the mainstream media in Britain and America.

Let us go back once more to the swan song of River Bend.

Saturday, 13 November 2004

Murder . . .

People in Fallujah are being murdered. The stories coming back are horrifying. People being shot in cold blood in the streets and being buried under tons of concrete and iron . . . where is the world? Bury Arafat and hurry up and pay attention to what's happening in Iraq.

They say the people have nothing to eat. No produce is going into the city and the water has been cut off for days and days. Do you know what it's like to have no clean water? People are drinking contaminated water and coming down with diarrhoea and other diseases. There are corpses in the street because no one can risk leaving their home to bury people. Families are burying children and parents in the gardens of their homes. WHERE IS EVERYONE?

Furthermore, where is Sistani? Why isn't he saying anything about the situation? When the South was being attacked, Sunni clerics everywhere decried the attacks. Where is Sistani now, when people are looking to him for some reaction? The silence is deafening.

We're not leaving the house lately. There was a total of 8 hours of electricity today and we've been using the generator sparingly because there is a mysterious fuel shortage . . . several explosions were heard in different places. Things are deteriorating swiftly.

Iraqis will never forgive this—never. It's outrageous—it's genocide and America, with the help and support of Allawi, is responsible. May whoever contributes to this see the sorrow, terror and misery of the people suffering in Fallujah.

A river that flows changes every moment with the water that flows through it, thereby taking on a new entity. This situation is not much different in *occupied Iraq*. Is that the reason why our protagonist in Iraq was forced to assume the pen name River Bend in the cyber world?

22 November 2004

Iraq war protest poster

5

PETROEURO: WEAPON THAT AMERICA FEARS

On 20 March 2006, just as America completes three years of Iraqi invasion, it is now targeting Iran, baptising it as central bank of terrorism.

Precisely because it is known that the much publicised rumour that Iraq has weapons of mass destruction was a fake allegation propagated by George Bush Jr, it would be impossible to believe that America is targeting Iran because of its developing nuclear power. The real crime that Iran committed is that it is located in one of the world's largest oil-producing regions. The allegations against Iran are the first steps against the 'axis of evil' which go against Bush Jr's decree that each drop of oil should flow through the sieves of America. The same mathematical calculations that went into the attack against Iraq, over and above the political significance of oil, can be seen behind the targeting of Iran as well. It is true that Iraq had weapons of mass destruction! But those were in the form of euro currency, and it is the same threat that Iran also uses against USA.

To understand the threat of euro, one must study the impact of dollar in the financial market. It is true that America, with its brawn power, would scare off any trade that challenged the supremacy of the dollar.

It was as a result of a treaty between America and the biggest oil-producing nation Saudi Arabia in 1973 that the dollar became the currency for oil trade. For this single reason, all nations need dollar to barter with the OPEC nations for oil. Those countries that fall back in furnishing the necessary percentage of dollar take huge loans from the IMF or the World Bank. This accounts for the huge demand for dollar outside America. Thus, America manages to increase its dollar deposit through means other than exports. Today, two-thirds of the world's economic exchange is based on dollar. Dollar is the foreign currency reserve of most nations. It is not just for the purpose of exchange of oil, but it will also help maintain steady money value for dollar. This is how the might of petrodollar has turned America into being a central bank that prints currencies welcomed in every nook and corner of the world. Due to the superiority attained by dollar in the international economy, America can manipulate and control the world market according to its whims and fancies.

If the OPEC nations severe bonds with dollar and switch over to euro, it will be a heavy blow to the economic supremacy of America. If so, nations around the world would gradually switch from dollar to euro as the foreign currency reserve, thereby increasing the deposit of euro and using it as the currency for international trade. This will lead to the decline of dollar and increase in value of euro. Economists point out that if a petroeuro system comes into existence, the value of dollar will fall from 20 per cent to 40 per cent in the world market. When Dr Mahathir Mohammed was the prime minister of Malaysia, he had requested all the Arab nations to come forward with a unified dinar currency to break free of the imperialistic rule of dollar over the trade of oil.

In 1999, when Iran tried to break away from dollar by establishing new ties with euro, America named it the axis of evil. It was Saddam Hussein who first implemented the petroeuro system in November 2000. Saddam used euro as the currency in UN's Food for Oil Programme as well. Saddam also converted Iraq's foreign currency reserve of 20 billion dollars in the UN to euro. Saddam wielding the petroeuro weapon amplified America's war plans against Iraq. Bush Jr envisaged that it would be a good lesson to countries like Iran, which are interested in the petroeuro system like Iraq. As Saddam implemented the petroeuro deal in the Gulf, dollar marked a depreciation of 17 per cent against euro in the world market in 2002.

One of the first things that Bush did after invading Iraq was re-establishment of the petrodollar system in oil deals. Besides, America also annulled all the oil deals that Saddam had established with China, Russia, and France during 1997-2002. The rupture of these deals, which had involved transactions to the rate of 1.1 trillion dollars, created rifts between America and other nations. From 2003, Iran has been using euro in the oil deals with the OPEC nations. This does agitate America. Iran has declared that an oil company in the model of the stock exchange, aimed at the marketing of oil from the OPEC nations and the sale of other petroleum products, would come into being this year. With this, Iran would move fully towards the petroeuro system. Although, from the case of Iraq, it may seem that there would be a military attack on Iran soon, there is little chance of America embarking on a direct plan of action. If we examine the direct invasions that America has carried out till date, we will find that all these were against nations without adequate power for self-defence. Hence, it is more plausible that Operation Ajax would be used against Iran.

The government of the Iranian Prime Minister Muhammad Mosaddegh had come into power through democratic elections in 1952. As soon as he assumed office, he nationalised Iran's oil sector. With this, Britain and America, who had lost control over Iran's oil, sabotaged the Iranian government in 1953 with the help of CIA and installed Shah, a puppet of America, as the ruler. This event, known as Operation Ajax, was discussed in detail by Stephen Kinzer, a reporter with *The New York Times*, in his book *All the Shah's Men*, published in 2003. America had sabotaged the Iranian government by bribing officials in high positions with the help of CIA and by organising street protests. Recently, it used the same tactics against the Venezuelan President Hugo Chávez.

Venezuela, a tiny Latin American country, stands fourth in the world in terms of oil production. Following Saddam's model, this anti-American country used euro instead of dollar in oil trade with thirteen Latin

American countries including Cuba in 2001. The angered America sabotaged Chavez's government in April 2002. But, within two days, Chavez regained power, surviving the military coup. Even now, America has not abandoned its plans of toppling Chavez's democratically elected government.

If Iran's oil exchange market comes into being, implementing the petroeuro system in all its totality, it would destroy the supremacy of London's International Petroleum Exchange (IPE) and New York's Mercantile Exchange (NYMEX); both are controlled by corporate giants in America. Bush Jr is a neo-fascist who won't hesitate to adopt any kind of despicable method to prevent Iran from implementing this move that can become a huge threat to America's dollar imperialism and then declare to the world that God had ordered him to carry out this mission.

If America's unabated thirst for control over the world's oil money leads to a war in this century, it can turn into a third world war, leading to the annihilation of the world as a whole. It is high time the Asian countries unite against America's murderous imperialist yearning to turn the entire Asian continent into a bloody battlefield.

26 March 2006

Saddam Hussein

Hugo Chávez during a tour of US Naval Ship

6

THE LATIN AMERICAN DAWN—THE INSPIRATION OF THE MIDDLE EAST

Remember Che Guevara's picture, the one that has been cherished by thousands of young people across the world as an icon of revolution?

Che, the Latin American guerrilla leader who overthrew the Cuban dictator Fulgencio Batista and thus brought Uncle Sam to his knees in the late Fifties, still remains the hero in young revolutionary minds. The picture of Che with his star-studded cap is the most popular picture in the world and remains a symbol of the twentieth century. Two years back, when I saw this picture on the cars of Arab youths, it had raised curiosity and amazement. This amazement ceased only when the news that Che's daughter was planning to take legal action against the trend of commodifying Che's pictures and inscribing it on products in the market came to be known.

Initially, it was thought that Arab youths had just taken a fancy for Che Guevara's picture, which had reached the Gulf market as a commodity. But this was not the case, as was revealed, when Al Jazeera reported several weeks back that along with the picture of Che, a picture of the Venezuelan President Hugo Chávez also appeared on the walls of Ramallah and Gaza, two regions considered as representing the general sentiments in the Arab streets. It was then that it was realised that this issue was more significant than as just an entertaining piece of news. It was with much zeal that Arab channels telecast visuals of the Venezuelan flag being raised along with those of Lebanon and Palestine in the protest demonstrations at Beirut and Palestine. Although references to Osama Bin Laden appear in Arab channels once in a while, he does not create much of a current in the Arab world. Just as more and more Americans have begun suspecting that the 11 September attacks were part of an American conspiracy, the Arab world believes that most of the statements supposedly being issued by Bin Laden are ones that favour America. Today Hugo Chávez is the hero of the Arab world. 'Today, most houses in Beirut are decorated with pictures of Che and Chavez.' This statement comes from none other than Syed Hassan Nasrallah, the leader of Hezbollah, which had emerged victorious in the Israel–Lebanon War.

If the imperialist interventions in the Middle East and Latin America are brought under study along with the anti-imperialist currents created by Latin American leaders in the Middle East, the similarities between these would surface. America's interventions in Latin America are as old as the very history of America. It was during the last three decades that this phenomenon became more complex. Today, Bush is practising in Latin America the new version of the very same imperialist strategies employed by President Ronald Reagan in the Eighties. The neo-realists, the evangelists, and the corporate masters who now assemble under Bush had then been supporting Reagan. During his reign, Reagan did his best to dismantle the communist–socialist ideals, which were a perpetual hindrance to the capitalist dream of a free-market economy. He made military interventions in Latin America under the pretext of freeing the Latin American population so that they could merge into the modern social order.

In the human hunts that America embarked upon to avenge the communists, the lives of over 70,000 innocent people in El Salvador, 100,000 in Guatemala, and 30,000 in Nicaragua were lost. Reagan expressed grief over the death of these innocent human beings but proclaimed to the world that such measures were essential to protect democracy and uphold human rights back then. The proclamations made by President Bush subsequent to the human genocides in Iraq and Afghanistan were in the same mould.

Today, leftist forces in Latin American countries are resurrecting themselves with renewed energy. The leftist socialist forces in Latin America, who have adopted the path of democracy, learning from the failure of the long bygone communist experiments and the collapse of the Soviet Union and from the tragedy of the socialist dream in Cuba, are in an attempt to free themselves from imperialist hegemony and give rise to a new spring. It is not just a little that America is agitated by the fact that from President Lula da Silva of Brazil to Argentina's Nestor Carlos Kirchner, Uruguay's Tabare Vazquez, Bolivia's Evo Morales, Chile's Veronica Michelle, and Venezuela's Hugo Chávez—all of whom came to power through elections –all are adherents of leftist socialism.

In Nicaragua as well, where the elections were held on 5 November, a staunch critic of America, Ortega, has come to power. Ortega is the fiery leader of the Marxist–Stalinist Liberation Front, which sabotaged Samoza, who had been the autocratic ruler wielding power with US support in the Eighties and seized power in Nicaragua through a people's revolution. During the presidency of Reagan, America had tried to destabilise Ortega by imposing economic sanctions and engaging contra-rebels against Nicaragua. America dreads the possibility of the formation of a Chavez–Ortega–Castro alliance, which may materialise if Ortega gains power through democracy. And that is why Paul Trivelli, the American ambassador to Nicaragua, has openly appealed to the people, discarding international principles, to vote against Ortega.

Forty per cent of the oil imports to America are from the Latin American countries like Venezuela, Mexico, Ecuador, and Columbia. From Venezuela alone, America imports 1.5 million barrels of oil (14 per cent) daily. Chavez's strategy of combating America with its own money has angered Bush. As per the reports of the *Petroleum Intelligence Weekly*, which is considered to be the Bible of the world of petroleum, the oil fields of Latin America, except those of Venezuela, are fast drying up. And oil will flow to America from these countries only for the next ten or fifteen years. On the other hand, as per the estimates of the US Department of Energy, the oil deposit in Venezuela is five times higher than that of Saudi Arabia. Bush knows pretty well that precisely because of this, Chavez will use oil as a weapon against America.

Chavez, declaring that Venezuela has nothing against US citizens, distributed 45 million litres of oil at 40 per cent reduction in the prices to the poor in America through Venezuela's Citgo Petrol Station networks in America. This act of charity from Chavez was equivalent to belittling Uncle Sam. Chavez has already given permission to distribute 100 million litres of oil to the poor in New York City. An American newspaper itself reported that through this scheme, 200,000 poor people, staying in 70,000 apartments in New York, can protect themselves from the severe winter cold at affordable rates (*New York Daily News*, 21 September 2006).

Through the Venezuelan experience, Chavez is showing the world that building up a welfare state with head held high, without demeaning oneself to the state of a lapdog of imperialism, is not a utopian dream. Precisely because of this, Hugo Chávez is on America's hit list. It was recently that Bush appointed the Deputy Director of CIA J. Patrick Meher as the manager of the Venezuela Mission in order to decide how to confront Chavez again after the failed attempt at sabotaging his government in 2002. North Korea and Iran are two other countries within the perimeters of such American mission managers.

It was not any Arab country but Chavez of Venezuela, miles away from the Arab world, which withdrew its ambassador from Tel Aviv as protest against Israel's attack on Lebanon. It was because of this that in the anti-war rally held at Kuwait, Arabs took to the streets with placards bearing Chavez's picture and the epithet 'True Arab Leader' beneath it. The famous speech 'Against the Devil' delivered on the soil of America turned Chavez into a popular leader in the global scenario. Chavez, leaving the podium after delivering the speech, told the media, 'The United States empire is on its way down, and it will be finished in the near future. Inshallah.' As Chavez says this the Arab way (ending the statement with the Arabic phrase for 'God willing'), he knows well that, more than anybody, it is the Arab populace who is waiting for the downfall of the empire.

13 November 2006

Palestinian boys wearing Che Guevara T-shirts

Che Guevara visiting Gaza Strip during 1959

7

AMERICA BECOMES A PAUPER!

Incredulous! But the writing is on the wall. American imperialism is nearing its end. What we are witnessing now is the declining slide of American authoritarianism, blazing arrogantly for one last time. That America's own National Intelligence Council (NIC) was among those who predicted the country's fall is a paradox of history.

A 119-page report titled 'Mapping the Global Future' issued by the NIC, which is a part of CIA, concludes that America's global dominance will likely end by 2020. If George Bush Jr does not, however, resign or is removed immediately, then Uncle Sam will be on his deathbed when the president's term ends in January 2009. The 'obituary report' indicates the following facts:

1. Germany and America dominated and controlled the world in nineteenth and twentieth centuries, respectively. The twenty-first century will belong to India and China, who will emerge as influential nations.

2. The tactics and strategies adopted by Brazil, Indonesia, and similar countries to isolate the United States will expedite its decline in international forums.

3. By 2020, Islam will be a resurgent political force, and the likelihood of a caliphate cannot be ruled out.

4. From its one-dimensional existence, the world order will turn multipolar in the near future.

What America now faces is similar to what the Soviet Union countenanced in the Eighties. While the USSR had all manners of arms and ammunitions to destroy the world, it became economically vulnerable, thus negating any military might that the country might have had. Even while the economic conditions were bad, they interfered militarily in Afghanistan. When the Soviet military's ten-year long battle with the Afghan Mujahideen did not succeed, they withdrew the forces from the country in 1989. Two years later, the world witnessed the decline of Soviet hegemony. A similar fate awaits the US in Iraq.

It was no less a personality than Henry Kissinger who mentioned in an interview to BBC that US will never succeed in Iraq. It is to be remembered that Kissinger was the foreign secretary under President Nixon during the Vietnam War and he is widely acclaimed as the Pope of American foreign policy. Tony Blair, in an interview to the English Channel of Al Jazeera, has already confessed that the Iraq War was a tragedy. This confession ought to be read along with Kissinger's statement. In another interview to CBS TV, President Bush admits that one of the hardest parts of his job is to connect Iraq to the War on Terror. In addition, he also indicated that if US cannot win this war at the ideological front, the result would be disastrous. Bush had reiterated this point in his address to the US Congress on 24 January. The reason is obvious. Unless Nouri Al Maliki, the US puppet in Iraq, is able to sanction the extraction of oil to American companies, the United States will be on a weak footing.

If the US fails in Iraq, Bush knows that the country would find it difficult to survive economically, which is why, as a clever tactic, the US has been able to project the Iraqi War as an anti-terror strike. But it must be realised that this war will take a massive toll on the US exchequer with an expenditure of nearly 2 trillion USD for this purpose. This would be a heavy burden for the American people to shoulder, as was declared by Joseph Stiglitz, a Nobel Laureate in economics.

It must be remembered that in 1945, when the Second World War ended, Britain was in a debt trap. History tells us that grand wars have set the stage for the decline of empires where the sun never set. It is common knowledge that America currently survives on foreign money. Fifteen per cent of the American economy is owed as debt to China. If China withdraws control of US Treasury receipts, it will be disastrous for the US. Once acclaimed to be the world's largest exporter and financier, the USA is turning out to be the world's biggest importer and debtor—a pathetic turnaround. The American Treasury Department's Web site indicates that the USA's overall debt is 8.6 trillion dollars.

Almost all countries export goods to the US, but not many of them import from the US in equal quantity. America's trade deficit with China is approximately 234,101 million dollars. While the US imports goods worth 287,774 million from China, what China imports from the US are only 53,673 million (source: www.census.gov). Reports also indicate that even with poorly developed countries like Ukraine, USA has a trade deficit. This imbalance in trade will open the doors of poverty. The only commodity that other countries can buy from the US is destructive weaponry, and that is why America is planting tensions across the world. As long as wars are perpetuated, America stands to gain.

The end of the twentieth century witnessed two power centres working conjointly to change the face of the world: one was America, and the other, the corporate agenda of globalisation. Ironically, even as the Iraq war exposes the limits of American superpowerdom, globalisation hasn't come to rescue it. While some giant US corporations flourish, the country is on the decline. The power of decision has consequently fallen into the hands of a few, converting America into an oligarchy.

As a result of globalisation, many US companies dealing in furniture, electronics, and automobiles have shifted their manufacturing centres to countries with lower wages and production costs. In the last five years, the US has lost 6,40,000 jobs in the IT sector alone. This works out to 17.4 per cent of the total IT workforce in the country. In the field of computer system designs alone, 1,05,000 people (8.5 per cent) lost their jobs. In the manufacturing sector, the figures are as follows:

- Communication equipment manufacturing—42 per cent
- Semiconductor components—37 per cent
- Electronic equipment—25 per cent
- Automobile spare parts—12 per cent

- Furniture industry—17 per cent
- Textiles—50 per cent

Between 2001 and 2006, nearly 2.9 million people lost their jobs in the manufacturing sector. This explosive situation has led to further divide between the rich and the poor in America. The middle class will soon vanish as they become consumed by poverty. This will lead to political instability and social unrest, resulting in the decline of the United States.

Boston University Professor Lawrence Kotlikoff points out that America, like its monopoly corporations like General Motors and Enron, is turning pauper. Kotlikoff, who was an advisor to IMF and the World Bank, has highlighted these conclusions in a research report prepared for the Federal Reserve. He goes on to say, in fact, that US is already a pauper.

With such a severe resource crunch and heavy debt, will America fall into poverty? This is the question that Kotlikoff raises. The financial health of many American financial companies and banks is pointed out to be weak and deplorable as indicated by David Walker, US financial expert, who pronounced that if some serious measures are not taken, America will be lured into an irreversible catastrophe.

29 January 2007

8

WILL OBAMA TURN INTO AMERICA'S GORBACHEV?

It was exactly two decades ago on 7 December 1988 that the then president of the Republic of Soviet Union, Mikhail Gorbachev, addressed the UN General Assembly and the world. Gorbachev announced that the Soviet Union would abandon the Brezhnev Doctrine and allow the Eastern Europe nations to freely determine their own internal affairs.

The compelling necessity of the principle of freedom of choice is also clear to us. The failure to recognize this, to recognize it, is fraught with very dire consequences, consequences for world peace. Denying that right to the peoples, no matter what the pretext, no matter what the words are used to conceal it, means infringing upon even the unstable balance that is, has been possible to achieve. Freedom of choice is a universal principle to which there should be no exceptions.

The whole of Soviet Union and Eastern Europe, who, for the major part of their country's history, were refused the right to vote, looked upon Mikhail Gorbachev with such promise and adoration, thinking that such a leader could bring voting freedom amongst them. Gorbachev paved the way for the end of dictatorship in Eastern Europe.Gorbachev proudly proclaimed to the Western world that they are no longer the target of Russian weapons. The world realised with wondrous amazement that Gorbachev's words were not just tall claims. The same Soviet Union, who enforced communist rule on Eastern Europe as a result of Warsaw Pact, comfortably backtracked from the Brezhnev ideals, which were their watchword long back from 1968.

One thing that remained evident throughout the entire length of the very famous UN speech was Gorbachev's confessions about the blunders he had committed and his deep, heartfelt remorse about his failure in reforming Soviet Union. He admitted that when there was financial downfall in the Soviet Union, they survived wielding their military might. But Gorbachev couldn't ignore the situation to continue like nothing has happened for longer periods of time. That era exhorted Gorbachev to take radically divergent views in political, economical, and foreign reforms, even though it resulted in a sea change in Russia's relationship with the world. To see his new theories and ideals in action, Gorbachev formulated action plans. If glasnost was the new method of dealing with the problems and issues through open discussion, perestroika was the quintessential reconstruction of the whole wagon wheel in the country's administrative machinery so as to court progress—both industrial and economical. But even Gorbachev's intervention was not enough to prevent destiny. In the beginning of the Nineties, fifteen republics proclaimed independence from the Soviet Union. Thus, USSR disappeared into thin smoke from among the nations in the world map.

As a result of Gorbachev's proclamation in the UN, the Soviet army retreated from Afghanistan, Hungary, East Germany, and Czechoslovakia, whereas Bush Sr repeated whatever mistakes Soviet Union was trying to correct. In 1989, the American army attacked Panama in the name of Operation Just Cause. Their next conquest was Afghanistan, a country shattered by war. It had become a burial ground as a result of foreign rule after foreign rule. Then came Iraq; it was a procession of mistakes. After a succession of ferocious wars and military invasions, America will very soon land itself in poverty.

As we have seen in the dying days of Soviet Union, it is only a cruel joke of history that the American people are facing the same trials and tribulations and Barack Hussein Obama, who has risen up amidst chaos as their saviour, reminds us of Mikhail Gorbachev. In an Italian publication, *La Stampa,* Gorbachev exhorted Obama to implement perestroika in America to redeem itself from the economic downfall that is crushing its progress day by day. Yet we have to look at it as the sad recurrence of a horrible truth in our past.

The data procured by US Department of Labour tell us that about 3.5 million Americans have lost their jobs last year. This year in January alone, 550,000 people lost their jobs. The reports from US census bureau this February suggest a serious downfall in the loan market. There is zero increase in the selling of house, but what is happening in the real estate market is the confiscation of houses due to non-repayment of loans. In the last financial year, 2 million had to leave their houses since they couldn't pay the instalments for their home loans. About 600 billion dollar is the loan deficit. Another 6 million more Americans will have to leave their homes if the same situation persists. News of group suicides, liquidation of banks, termination notice for employees, and company closures are being circulated all around America.

In Obama's constituency, Chicago's 74,000 people are destitute and homeless. The homeless have now established rows of *tents* in cities like Trino in Chicago, USA, making them *tent cities* if we can believe a recent report by BBC. Fifty million people are finding it extremely difficult to make both ends meet even when they have a job, says the Centre for Economic and Policy Research Report. Very soon, American cities will be suffocating with millions of jobless youth, and within a short span of time, they will exhaust their savings. Vallejo, a municipality in California, has proclaimed officially that they are paupers. They are finding it difficult to procure funds to run the day-to-day activities of the municipality and pay the staff. There are quite a few municipalities in the US who are awaiting to be proclaimed pauper by the US government.

In certain corners of America, some citizens are raising difficult questions: who are the actual beneficiaries of the federal establishment in the United States and is the establishment in place capable enough to take care of the diverse needs of its people? Thought-provoking questions emerging from America are a refreshing sight, and it may be the beginning of the urge for a different establishment. There are fifty different nations under fifty flags, which are recognised as fifty republics. There are basically right-wingers who call themselves the blue states, and the socialist left-wingers who proudly name themselves the red states. The differences existing in ideology, policy making are escalating between the red and blue states day by day. In the biggest state of America, Alaska, the desire for freedom is at its peak. The organisation which is working for the liberation of Alaska, Alaskan Independence Party, is the third biggest political force in Alaska. The fact that the governor of Alaska, and the nominee of the Republican Party for the post of vice-president, Sara Paulin, has strong and irrefutable links with Alaskan Independence Party, as reported by a New York newspaper during the last presidential elections. Alaska is the province that America bought from Russia in 1867 at the rate of two cents per acre. That bargain cost America a whole of 2 million dollars, thereby buying Alaska and making it the forty-ninth state of the USA. The sea cost of Russia and Alaska is only 5 km apart. So America fears that if Alaska gets its independence, it may turn out to be a satellite country of Russia.

In yet another state, California, the movement of freedom is visible. The organisation which is at the forefront of the freedom movement is the Nation of Aztlan. California is the state that pays the lion's share of the amount of money in a year's taxes to the federal government. But the Hollywood actor-turned Governor Arnold Schwarzenegger feels that the development in infrastructure taking place in California is disproportionate.

Another major issue that is affecting the American psyche is the political unrest in Mexico. In Mexico, which is under the rule of drug kingpins, kidnapping and beheading of officials are rampant. The drug mafia exports weapons from America to Mexico and thereby paves way for the free transport of miscreants and drug addicts to the country. Thus, Mexico creates alarming threat to the internal security of the people of USA, and this is a thorn in Obama's attempt at smooth governance. If the former presidents had to content with international issues, Obama has to face the internal repercussions of those issues.

Whatever the reason be, when the United States (US) is going along the same path travelled by the Soviet Union (SU), you don't have to be a great thinker to see that the repercussions of Obama's actions are the same as that of Gorbachev's.

06 March 2009

Mikhail Gorbachev

Barack Hussein Obama

9

AMERICAN IMPERIALISM: A MENACE WHILE BREATHING ITS LAST!

When America stoops from its pedestal as a world power, a lot of questions and issues emerge from all around the world. How will this depletion of power affect the dollar, which is the foreign currency reserve of the whole world? Who will emerge as the leader in this new economic power struggle? Will America be able to threaten the world even when it is in the verge of disintegration?

The Telegraph reported that the G20 nations, while expecting the downfall of dollar, are trying to support the world economy from its aftermath by formulating a new world currency under the direct surveillance of the World Bank ('G20 Moves the World a Step Closer to Global Currency, *The Telegraph*, 4 April 2009). From 1945 onwards, dollar is enjoying the privilege of being the foreign currency reserve of the whole world. As the speculation began that the value of dollar is on an all-time low, the nations which were using dollar as a foreign currency reserve began to panic.

China that has 2 trillion dollar foreign currency reserve expressed its frustration quite openly. The lion's share of Chinese deposits is US treasury bonds, which increase the seriousness of their problem. It is high time the world decides on an alternative world currency other than dollar, says an annual review by the Chinese Central Bank. This issue was reported by *The Financial Express* on 27 June 2009 in its article titled 'China Harps on a New World Currency'. As India's reserve currency with World Bank is 264 billion dollars, it came out in open defiance of America together with Russia and China to question the dominance of dollar in the global financial market. In preparation of the G8 summit in Italy last July, Indian prime minister's Economic Advisory Chairman Suresh Tendulkar made some adverse remarks against America. *The Financial Express* gave this news wide coverage with the title 'Now India Questions Dollar Dominance' (6 July 2009).

If America's economy breaks down completely like that of Iceland and Latvia, it will shake up the whole world's economy. All the experts have predicted that the economic meltdown is going to happen in the near future. A member of the monetary policy committee and advisor of many famous financial institutions and world governments and a professor of London School of Economics, Willem Buiter asserts that between two and five years from now, there will be a global dumping of US dollar assets, including US government assets.

At a time when the US economy undergoes crisis, the billions of dollars spent by them to back up the overseas military bases are soon going to be a financial burden for America. According to an official annual report by *The Pentagon* in 2008, the military camps established by the USA are spread around 865 units across 150 countries. These state-of-the-art military camps are not at all meant for defending the security of the country but serving the territorial ambitions of USA. The expenditure to maintain these camps is quite huge, says the Director of National Priorities Project Research Director Anita Danks. As per her report, the cost of the global US military presence is 250 billion dollars ('Foreign Policy in Focus', 6 July 2009, page 91). It will be better for America if they follow the path of Britain as they stop being a colonial superpower and realise the pitfalls of maintaining a military empire. It is easier said than done. It is likely that the vast military empire controlled by the US and spread around various nations in the world is likely to be under the command of UN—as it is being put forward as an alternative world government with the backing of USA.

The BRICS nations are looked upon as a centre of power by some political observers. The first summit of these nations was held in Russia on 16 June 2009, but since Uncle Sam is not ready to let anyone else take over as the king of the power chain, they may find an alternative in the name of UN under their nose that they can easily manipulate.

Strobe Talbott, whom Bill Clinton nominated him as America's deputy secretary of the state (1994-2001), has written a very thought-provoking article 'Birth of a Global Nation' in *The Times* magazine years ago. The core idea goes like this: within the next 100 years, the term *country* will lose its meaning. Nations will cease to exist, forming a global nation. Nowadays, the term *global citizen* is in fashion. This term will come into reality in the middle of twenty-first century (*The Times*, 20 July 1992). This was the idea perpetuated by Strob Talbott's article. In 1998, he wrote an elaborate textbook *The Great Experiment: The Story of Ancient Empire Modern States and the Quest for a Global Nation.*

Zbgniew Brzeznski is another think tank who upholds the global nation theory with America being the epicentre of power. He has served President Ronald Regan. Brzeznski is the founding father of the trilateral commission, working towards forming a global government. He came forward in open support of Obama during the last presidential election. His book *The Second Chance: The Presidents and Crisis of American Superpower* is seen by many as the struggle of America to re-establish imperialism around the world. As per the *Washington Post*, this book will become President Obama's manifesto ('A Manifesto for the Next President', *Washington Post*; 14 March 2007).

Gerald Celente is an American Trend forecaster and the director of Trend Research Institute in New York. He is seen by many as the Nostradamus of America and was described as future prediction expert by BBC, CNN, and *New York Times*. He analysed that the lack of morality in Americans is the core cause of current issues haunting America. He correctly predicted 1987 stock market downfall and the 1997 Asian currency crisis. His viewpoints and analysis on current affairs in US are interesting. Following are his observations:

Wall Street is managed by thugs. They want to know how much one can grab from someone else's wealth. They act as if they are getting benefited from a jackpot. The government's regulations also support this to a large extent. To escape the economic restraints that America is facing nowadays, if the Obama government is thinking in the line of printing dollar, the situation will go from bad to worse. The downfall of the real estate market will lead to depreciation of dollar so that it will become useless commodity.

Gold is one such deposit which is always valuable. Soon the price of one ounce of gold will reach to 2,000 dollars (current price is $957). The percentages of jobless people in US have increased to 25 per cent. When they feel that, they would have lost everything and would resort to violence. Organisation for Economic Cooperation and Development (OECD), an international organisation with more than thirty branches all over the world and has its headquarters at Paris, gives out the valuable headcount that there is significant increase in the number of those who have not completed their high school education. They end up in drug lobbies being drug addicts. Gerald thinks that those people who are separatists in America will lead them in the same direction as Soviet Russia. Humanevents.com, a famous Web portal while talking to Gerald Celente, bluntly asked their last question: 'How will it all end? Will the dollar survive?'

Here is Celente's very sharp reply:

The dot com bubble should have burst and gone away in a short sharp recession. But the boys at the Fed re-inflated the economy by lowering interest rates to a 46 year low—and in turn created the real estate bubble—much bigger than the dot com bubble.

Now they're creating the bailout bubble—which will ultimately dwarf the real estate bubble. It will cause the implosion of the global economy world wide—which will not be able to be repaired by creating yet another bubble. Every time the government fails, it tells a bigger lie and then a still bigger lie.

These previous bubbles were not allowed to pop—but they didn't destroy the infrastructure of the country. This bailout bubble will.

But this bubble will be the last one. After the final blowout of the bailout bubble, we are concerned that the government will take the nation into war. This is a historical precedent that's been done over and over again.

So, it's not that the dollar that will survive. We may not even survive. Look at the German mess after WWI. It gave rise to Fascism and WWII. The next war will be fought with weapons of mass destruction (humanevents.com; 6 May 2009).

We cannot just dismiss Gerald Celente's view as a crank conspiracy theory. America was converted into a white continent, using desperate war measures, says history. During 1754-63, the white generation who came to America as the first settlers used small pox against the Red Indians in the first ever instance of biological warfare known to man. Thus, they cleansed America of Red Indians as much as they could, so Americans have the dubious history of ethnic cleansing against the Red Indians.

The Americans have a blackened past, but they can't do away with it in the present too. Thousands of samples of bacterial agents that cause deadly diseases like plague, anthrax, and tularaemia; Venezuelan, Eastern and Western equine encephalitis viruses; rift valley fever virus; Junin virus; Ebola virus; botulinum neurotoxins; and virus of other communicable diseases have been kept in the US Army Medical Research Institute of Infectious Diseases at Fort Detrick, Md., says *Global Security Newswire* in association with the centre's Deputy Commander Col. Mark Kortepeter.

The year 2001 was the beginning of the anthrax scene that kept the US in the forefront of a biological warfront episode that started such scares all around the world. A former USAMRIID (United States Army Medical Research Institute of Infectious Diseases) Researcher Bruce Ivins was responsible for the 2001 anthrax mailings that killed a few people. Later, the prime suspect Microbiologist Bruce Ivins was found dead in July 2008 in suspicious circumstances as federal prosecutors prepared charges against him (*Global Security Newswire*; 18 June 2009). Imperialism has unveiled its last weapon in its armorial biological warfare. This has come as a huge scare to the world. Uncle Sam is thinking in these lines: 'If I'm going down, I will take the whole world with me too.'

19 July 2009

10

ARAB SPRING AND THE SHIFTING WORLD ORDER

The major question that baffled political scientists during the Nineties when the Cold War came to a close was what the nature of the world order about to be ushered in would be and also as to the source of political animosities in the future. It was Samuel P. Huntington, a professor at Harvard University, who came out with an answer to this much-discussed question. The crux of the Huntington theory, which categorised the world into eight civilisations on the basis of geographical locations, was that the current world order would be dominated by the clash of Islamic civilisations with Western ones. The article, which appeared in 1993 in America, in *Foreign Affairs*, was expanded in 1997 and published as a book titled *The Clash of Civilisations and the Making of World Order*. Although it has been two years since Huntington died, his eighteen-year-old theory is still the defining factor for America to formulate its global policies on redrawing the map of the Middle East, even during this era of the Arab Spring.

Huntington, who exerted a great influence on the policy formulation of the American government, had borrowed his doctrine from Bernard

Lewis, the godfather of orientalism. It was Bernard Lewis who first prophesied that Islam and the West would be at loggerheads with each other and termed it the clash of civilisations in his article 'The Roots of Muslim Rage', which appeared in 1990 in the *Atlantic Weekly*. Again, the caricature which was claimed to be that of Prophet Muhammad appeared for the first time, not in the Danish newspaper but in Bernard Lewis's book *The Middle East: A Brief History of the Last 2000 Years*, written in 1996.

Even before the former American President George Bush Jr turned eloquent on the policies regarding the Middle East, Bernard Lewis, who had also been his political advisor, had, in his book *The Emergence of Modern Turkey* (1961), upheld Turkey as a model for the whole of the Middle East. Bernard Lewis had argued that the reforms Ataturk had brought about in Turkey should be implemented across the Middle East. Ataturk's reforms included shutting down the madrasas, which imparted religious education, removing the Arabic scripts in Turkish and also anything that was linked to Islamic culture and banning headdresses.

As John L. Esposito, the political commentator and a professor in America's George Town University, critiqued, it was the honourable Jewish papa, Bernard Lewis, engaged in studying history even at the late age of ninety-five, who was responsible for America's wrong-footed policies. The responses of Bernard Lewis, the man upheld by the Western media as the guardian of the Middle Eastern history, towards current issues may seem like cruel jokes. Lewis remarked about the revolt of the youth against the corrupt governments in the Middle East:

> One has to remember that in the Muslim world, casual sex, Western-style, doesn't exist. If a young man wants sex, there are only two possibilities—marriage and the brothel. You have these vast numbers of young men growing up without the money, either for the brothel or the bride price, with raging sexual desire. On the one hand, it can lead to the suicide bomber, who is attracted by the virgins of paradise that is one reason why they are ready to enter the battlefield and embrace martyrdom ('A Mass Expression of Outrage against Injustice', *The Jerusalem Post*, 25 February 2011).

In reality, the trademarks of the successful mass protests in Tunisia and Egypt were discipline and non-violence. In a way, what the Arab Christian thinker Edward Said said is right: the conflicts in the world from now on will be within civilisations. That is what the Middle East hears as the thunder of spring.

Bernard Lewis is of the opinion that as it was democracy that brought Hamas and Hezbollah into power in Gaza and Lebanon, respectively, Western-style democracy is not desirable in the Middle East. It was because of the very same reasons that the Arab Spring, which endeavoured to impart power to the people, did not find support from America.

But there are some historical reasons for America taking a different approach towards Libya. The military head Col. Muammar Gaddafi had seized power after deposing King Idris, who was America's pet, just as the Shah of Iran, through a bloodless coup. Immediately after seizing power in 1969, he annulled the earlier contract that sanctioned military bases for America. Besides, with the nationalisation of the oil companies in 1973, the American oil companies had to head out from Libya. It was America's all-time necessity to oust Gaddafi, who was a threat to their interests. But America also realises that the Arab Spring blowing in the Middle East is a threat to them too. Although the Arabian Spring, which carried with it the Jasmine Revolution in Tunisia and the Nile Revolution in Egypt, will not seep into the strongest economic region, which is the source of energy for the entire world, from Syria, it is essential for America to turn it in their favour so that their political and economic ambitions won't be affected. That is why they did away very surreptitiously with the global terrorist Osama bin Laden, who they themselves had fostered in the very land they sang lullabies to and dumped his body in the sea without much ado at the most opportune time. It is sure that now the plot of the pre-planned script of the global stage drama would be altered. New words will take the place of terms like *Muslim ire*, *the clash of civilisations*, *Islamic terrorism*, and so on. It is highly essential for America to come up with novel storylines to weave political strategies that would suit the fast-changing world order. And the successors of Huntington, Bernard Lewis, and Francis Fukuyama, who circle Obama now, must be busy formulating policies accordingly.

8 June 2011

Bernard Lewis

US President Barack Obama and Vice-President Joe Biden, along with members of the national security team, receive an update on Operation Neptune's Spear, a mission against Osama bin Laden, in one of the conference rooms of the White House Situation Room on 1 May 2011. They are watching live feed from drones operating over the bin Laden complex

11

COLLAPSING CAPITALISM, SWELLING MASS ANGER

The past few decades have seen the emergence of an *elite* group under the auspices of the capitalist system, more influential than any other on the earth. The members of this group have managed to exert a constant influence on the lives of the 6 billion people all over the world. David Rothkopf, who has done a detailed study on the phenomena, says that this order has almost 6,000 members, including heads of states, media giants, billionaire directors of monopolised companies, technological and industrial entrepreneurs, diplomats, and even the heads of terrorist organisations. All of them have reaped gains by policy formulation in tandem with the stances of America, the capitalist paradise. Even as the very survival of America took the shape of the formula business through camouflaged politics of war on terror from the former one of business through war, those in the corporate sector, including the above-mentioned elite class, were reaping profits.

The world has now realised the hollowness and fallacy of American capitalism. In the *elite* section, it was the transnational corporations that reaped huge financial successes. It is estimated that, as of now, the total asset of 2,000 corporate monopolies is 103 trillion dollars and their annual sale, 27 trillion dollars. Almost 70 million people work in these companies. Assuming that there are 4 people reliant on each of these workers, it can be said that 350 million people get their livelihood from these corporate companies. If the contracts the corporate companies make with other small-scale companies are also brought into the picture, the number of job opportunities will be even higher. The decisions of a few thousand people, including the management and members of the boards of these corporate companies, have a marked impact on the lives of 1 billion or more. On another side, as 4 billion people struggle to make ends meet, corporate agendas make their lives bleaker, directly or indirectly.

Eighty-five per cent of the share market investments in America are under the control of the rich 10 per cent of the population. Forty per cent of America's wealth is in the hands of the very rich who constitute 1 per cent of the population of the country. As the nation called America plunges down to the economic level of the Third World countries, the American corporate giants are fattening. Things are moving towards a crisis graver than the Great Depression of 1929. As the world has turned into a free market today, thanks to globalisation, all countries will have to bear the consequences of the economic crisis. Even the propagators of the free market have recognised it to be a *corporatist* trap set by a small percentage of people with vested interests. American capitalism had set forth the promise that anyone who toils hard can climb any height. But what the world saw was the gap between the haves and the have-nots widening as capitalism gained strength.

Along with America, all the European countries, following the capitalist system, are in a huge financial crisis. As life became miserable, tens of thousands of people in America and Europe have taken to the streets in protest of the government and the corporates. It is the approval that the Arab Spring had received from the masses through social media that functions as inspiration for the spreading of mass ire towards capitalism in America and Europe. Like in the case of the mass uprisings during the Arab Spring movements, there are no leaders or leadership to be seen in anti-corporate leagues. Social networking sites are used in all the countries involved to gather mass support. People took to the streets of Manhattan in protest of America's economic policies, corporate greed, and policy-formulation lobbies under the label 'Occupy Wall Street' on 17 September. It is spreading like a cyclone to American cities and Europe, including London and Rome, as a protest against the capitalist system. In Italy, the protest turned violent. There were *occupy* protest demonstrations in Australia, Germany, New Zealand, Spain, Taiwan, and Philippines. Like in the Arab Spring, scenes of demonstrators settling down near traffic squares with readymade tents can be seen in cities like London. The banners and posters they hold make evident how bleak life has become for the masses under the capitalist system. The results of the Rasmussen National Telephone Survey reveal that 79 per cent of the American population is in support of the protest.

People around the globe are in fear of corporates tightening their hold on governments. The mass anger all over the world against corporates is a result of the realisation that as capitalism self-annihilates, it is necessary to curb corporate encroachment.

19 October 2011

Occupy Wall Street protesters at Zuccotti Park in Lower Manhattan near Wall Street

12

ALARMING BELLS FOR THE FUTURE OF TOMORROW

The world is at a historical turning point. The global movements from now on may not appear before us as issues related to terrorism or war. As the fragrance of democracy is spreading over the Middle East, capitalism is keeling over in the West. As quite a few fear if the democracy, which has recently set its foot in the Middle East, would pave the way for theocracy, the number of those who have misgivings as to whether the West will soon be under the iron grip of *corporatocracy* is not any less. The last year bore witness to America and Europe losing confidence in their tomorrow and the world's fondness for them diminishing owing to the collapse of their economies. The past years also saw people all over the world joining hands against economic inequality and corruption.

In this context, the Occupy Wall Street movement, which started off as an anti-monopoly protest against the widening economic equality between the 1 per cent of the population, who control the American economy and the rest 99 per cent, is attracting global attention. In the olden days, emperors and kings used to resort to rumour propagation in order to divert the attention of the masses from the real issues. Even today, not only political leaders and heads of states but monopolised media also wield the same weapon to protect their interests. The fact that the ire against economic inequality seeped into the West from the Middle East, which had been an area turned notorious through the above-said weapon, as a wholesale seller of terrorism, must be a historical destiny.

Towards the anti-monopoly protests, the mainstream media across the globe have been indifferent at first and then have adopted a couldn't-care-less attitude. As per Wikipedia statistics, the Occupy movement against the capitalist system has been gaining strength in ninety cities, including Sidney, Hong Kong, Taipei, Paris, Berlin, Tokyo, Paulo, Madrid, and Hamburg, besides the cities in the US. In this movement against the unholy alliance between corporates and the government, the protestors have adopted the strategies of the revolutionary Arab Spring and the Gandhian methods of protest. The protestors, who have begun settling down in tents set up in the streets, are exhorting people to renounce goods from the malls of monopolised companies like Walmart and to stop consumption of unessential items. It is the realisation that curbing the encroachment by the corporates which are tightening their grasp on governments is essential for a balanced social order, which prompts the Occupy protestors to take such decisions. The anti-monopoly protestors proclaim to the world that if the corporates are not brought under control, they would undo the ecological balance, as well as economic stability, and that they would turn into power centres more powerful than governments. Their words echo the apprehension that the world would fall into the hands of *corporatocracy*.

If the current system, which exploits public property, as well as natural resources, persists, the rich countries of the world would vanish and, instead, wealth would accumulate in the hands of a small section of the population in the near future. A comparison between the economic levels of multinational monopolised companies and governments yields astonishing results. The global turnover of ExxonMobil in 2007 was higher than the total domestic production of Saudi Arabia. That of Walmart surpassed the production in Indonesia and Poland. The same year, the overall turnover of the first 250 companies of the world outranked the total domestic production of America and Europe.

As per statistics, in 2007, there were only 60 countries in the list of the biggest economic giants in the world. The rest 106 were multinational monopolies.

Over the years, the corporates exerted a great influence on governments, and so, as countries all over the world faced financial crisis, the multinational monopolies fattened day by day. Even as the nation called America became bankrupt, no kind of financial crisis affected corporate America. The profit made by American corporate companies in 2010 was an all-time record ('Corporate Profits Rate Rise to Record Annual Rate', *Wall Street Journal*, 24 November 2010). The corporates had created their own lobbyists by offering attractive jobs to the family members of heads of states, government officials, and highly powerful people in the military after their retirements so that policies conducive to them (the corporates) would be adopted.

In his work *So Damn Much Money* released recently, Robert Kaiser has brought to light shocking information about corporate lobbying in America. Kaiser reveals with an array of evidence the fact that 42 per cent of the House members, half of the senators during the period from 1998-2004, 310 officials during the George Bush government, and 283 during Clinton's time were lobbyists. It is to such shocking reports that the world bears witness today. The coming days would see in all clarity many a hidden truth coming to light.

1 January 2012

13

LESSONS FROM THE MIDDLE EAST

It has to be feared that the current issues plaguing the Middle East would have deep and widespread consequences in economic, political, and security ties on the global stage. But most of us are uninterested in discussing the Syrian issue or the Iran problem. It seems that we have been seized by the misconception that this concern with foreign affairs is the work of certain specialists and those who waste time eavesdropping on neighbours instead of looking after one's own household, as P. Govinda Pillai remarked once.

Most people associate the Middle East solely with Iraq, bomb explosions, and so on. For some, the Middle East brings to mind the Israel–Palestine issues and news related to the Arab world. The Middle East is a terrain, where, besides the Arabs, a large number of races like the Armenians, the Assyrians, the Baha'is, the Berbers, the Chaldeans, the Copts, the Darsis, the Ibadis, the Ismaelis, the Jews, the Kurds, the Maronis, the Sahrawis, the Turkmens, the Yassids and the Saids, reside. This place was far ahead of Europe in terms of urbanity and civilisation even before 5,000 years till five centuries back. This is also the epicentre of Semitic religions like Judaism, Christianity, and Islam. History says that it was the Babylonian king Hammurabi who codified a system of law, comprising a number of topics, eighteen centuries before Christ. Other than the Arab countries including Saudi Arabia, the Middle East comprises Egypt, Libya, Sudan, Yemen, Jordan, Morocco, Tunisia, Palestine, Israel, Lebanon, Syria, Turkey, Iraq, and Iran.

As the West came to be highly exalted in historical and geographical descriptions, the Middle East was often projected by the Occident as uncivilised. In *The Principal Dogmas of Orientalism*, Edward Said describes it as follows:

Orientalist historiographers portrayed the West as rational, developed, humane, and superior. They depicted the Orient as aberrant, undeveloped and inferior, living according to set rules inscribed in sacred texts. About the Orient, they remark that the people do not live according to the changing demands of life.

Although Edward Said's book is dated 1978, these dogmas are still alive.

The Middle Eastern countries are in the process of a radical change. In December 2010, the Arab Spring hit this region in much the same way as the 1989 Eastern European Revolution against communist countries. It was the suicide of a young fruit seller in Tunisia that gave life breath to the revolution against the social order. It spread from Tunisia to Egypt, Yemen, Libya, and Syria. In all these countries, except Syria, the governments collapsed. As, after the elections, Islamist parties came into power in Egypt and Tunisia—in Libya, after the election—Mohamed al-Magariaf, who has been able to maintain amicable relationships with the Islamists, has become the interim president. The revolution did not affect the Arab countries precisely because the rulers maintain good ties with the people and endeavour to raise their standard of living. After all, revolutions take birth when, due to economic deterioration, the lives of the masses turn bleak.

The current politics in the Middle East cannot be analysed independent of America. Because, after the cold war, the Middle East has become the battlefield of imperialism. The main reason behind this is the interest in the oil fields. Another reason is the Israel–Palestine conflict in this region. But the imperialist–Zionist axis has succeeded in propagating the notion that Iran is the biggest security threat to this region in recent times. This alliance is trying its best to use the

Shia–Sunni conflict to their advantage. The Iran–America relationship is worsening day by day, owing to the fracas over developing nuclear energy in Iran. It was against this background that, on 4 August, the short-range missile Fatah, developed by Iran, was tested. The outbreak of the news that as a response to it, Israel has set up Arrow 2 Block 4 missiles around its border is creating unrest in the Middle East. America had recently given 70 million dollars to Israel as assistance for the missile project. As America gifted Israel with weapons to counter the *threat* from Iran, it also transacted the world's largest weapon sale of 60 billion dollars with other countries in the region. America's unholy alliance with Israel has often propelled the growth of political extremism in this region.

The Arab Spring has presented both challenges and opportunities to American interest in the Middle East. Precisely because the imperialist attempts to export democracy to Iraq through military intervention hit back at America financially and politically, it is following a cunning new trick in the case of the Middle East. Though no one would opine that Saddam Hussein was a total saint, he was definitely a ruler who endeavoured to raise the standard of living of the masses financially and through scientific progress. During Saddam's reign, no riots took place among tribes or religious sects in Iraq. In the eight-year war against Iran, 80 per cent of the people in Saddam's military were Shias, even as Saddam himself was a Sunni Muslim. But today, this country is going through Sunni–Shia conflicts and racial riots. In the last months, the number of people who fell dead in the explosions which took place over the course of a single day in Iraq was 104. The American military had bid adieu after creating an autonomous region called Kurdistan in Iraq where even the basic facilities were in tatters. This was part of the agenda to maintain Iraq as a problem-ridden region forever.

When America kept its distance, not intervening in any way in the protests in Egypt and Tunisia since they were against imperialist interests, they are assisting the protestors indirectly in Libya and now in Syria. It cannot be determined whether Bashar al-Assad is better or worse than Saddam Hussein. Just as both of them belonged to the Bath Party, both of them were merciless in the way they dealt with their enemies. Even during the time when the country called Israel came into being after exiling the Palestinians in 1948, the relationship between America and Syria was worsening. The former American President Bush Jr used to refer to Syria as a rogue nation. Political observers have already prophesied that after Iraq, Syria will be America's next prey. The strange phenomenon of the Al-Qaeda fighters, along with the Syrian Liberation Army fighting against Bashar's rule, with the support of America and its allies, is unfolding in Syria now. Recently, the American Defence Secretary Leon Panetta had openly confessed that the Al-Qaeda as well is on a mission to topple the Syrian government. As the Al-Qaeda, which Ronald Reagan had called during the war against Russia in Afghanistan 'the moral equivalents of America's Founding Fathers', is once again turned by America into their weapon in Syria, it is the mask of Uncle Sam's anti-terrorist movement that is falling off. The Council on Foreign Relation (CFR), a think tank, which has a major influence on America's foreign affairs policy formulation says that without Al-Qaeda's help, the Syrian dissenters would be nothing. Russia and China have vetoed almost three resolutions against Syria, which have been brought to the UN till now. It has to be feared if the revolt against Bashar in Syria, which has been continuing for almost seventeen months, would finally turn the Middle East into a Sunni–Shia conflict area.

Kofi Annan, who had been in charge of the Syrian Peace Plan, had requested the revolutionaries to stall the protests in Syria, which were causing large-scale bloodshed and massacres, and prepare themselves for talks. But they were unwilling for any compromise less than Bashar's resignation. Finally, owing to the lack of support for his attempts, Kofi Annan resigned from the UN peace mission. On 2 August, leaving his post as special envoy to Syria, he put forth some suggestions to solve the crisis in Syria ('My Departing Advice on How to Save Syria', *Financial Times*, 2 August 2012). These instructions deserve attention. The crux of Annan's message is that if Bashar is ousted without reaching a political formula, taking everybody in the region into confidence, Syria will be pushed into racial revolts, thereby propelling the Middle East into a great tragedy and that the world would have to face its repercussions.

There is a joke that gained popularity in Egypt during the Arab Spring:

Seeing the protest demonstrations taking place in Tahrir Square, the military commander told the Egyptian President Hosni Mubarak, 'Dear

President, it seems that everything is about to end. You should prepare a farewell speech to be addressed to the people.'

Mubarak replied, 'Oh! Really? Where are they going?'

Hosni Mubarak need not always be the protagonist of this comic story.

16 August 2012

Hosni Mubarak

Tahrir Square during the 2011 Egyptian Revolution

14

THE WORLD LEADS TO A CURRENCY WAR

It was by the last decade of the twentieth century that the economic scenario became globalised. Though multinational companies had been in existence for decades, with globalisation, they were transformed into global corporations. Totally abandoning the essence of the country in which they were located, they turned into a new global brand. These companies determine the prices of their products and the value of shares, based not only on the production costs in a country but also on the basis of the purchasing value of currency in many other countries.

Today, although the possibility for customers to choose products is available across the world, this is not accessible for everybody. Similarly, at the global level, the distribution of natural resources is also unequal. It is a reality that, owing to these reasons, globalisation has led to the spread of inequality in the world. Although the advocates of capitalism asserted that it would be the capitalist social order that would control the global market, this also, like the arguments of autocrats, imperialist powers, and communists, did not have the back-up of history. If future history marks the end of the twentieth century with the collapse of the Soviet

Union, the birth of the twenty-first century took place amid talks of the bankrupt global capitalism.

If the recent prophecies are to be believed, the global economic scenario, although out of the intensive care unit, is still under complete observation in the hospital ward. It is a well-known fact that the global economic order began swaying with the collapse of Lehman Brothers in the banking sector in America on 15 September 2008. The economic crisis, which led to losses of a total of 13 trillion dollars in the US housing sector and loss of employment for 6 million people within one year, spread from America, the origin of the global capitalist social order, to other countries of the world.

The world is passing through days which reveal that the world's greatest economic empires are, in reality, stark naked. Economic experts point out that the US economic order is on the tip of the sword between economic depression and inflation. But since it is not sure for how much time it can be balanced like this, the heartbeat of depositors and businessmen across the world is increasing day by day. Nation states are also under the shadow of trepidation since the collapse of the US dollar can topple the global economic sector. Jim Yong Kim, the president of the World Bank, warns that if countermeasures are not taken, the economic crisis would spread to the developing countries as well.

But the US Federal's decision to go for an uncontrolled minting of dollar in order to deal with the severe economic depression and increasing unemployment would have consequences all over the world. This move should be seen as the announcement of a currency war over the world.

The European countries, swaying in the wake of the economic crisis, would affect the most by such a move. Since the value of euro is becoming higher than that of dollar, the export prices of European products have increased. This increase in prices in the global market has become an impediment to their attempts to come out of the economic crisis. The minting of dollars would lead to inflation in China, rise of food prices, and increasing unemployment in developing countries like India. Depositors in the US blame China for reducing the value of their currency (yuan) much earlier, which led to a reduction in the prices of their products in the global market, as a result of which the American industrial production sector weakened, leading to massive loss of employment.

Bringing down the value of the currency of a country through artificial means to levels lower than that of countries engaged in trade relations with it would, as per economic principles, create extremely perilous consequences.

Although reduction in the value of currency would help raise exports and gain temporary economic growth, if the countries engaged in trade relations with this particular country take countermeasures, the finale of the currency wars would be totally unpredictable. In the conference of the BRICS (Brazil, Russia, India, China, South Africa) nations held last September, the finance minister of India, Pranab Mukherjee, had given the warning that the world is moving towards a currency war. He had appealed to the international community not to cut down the currency value in competition with each other but rather to find solutions to problems through dialogue. The reason for the economic crisis in the countries of Asia and Latin America in 1997 was the competitive currency wars between these countries. At that time, Indonesia, Malaysia, Thailand, and North Korea were sanctioned financial help as part of the US aid scheme. But, later, America propelled them into such a situation that they had no option other than reduce currency value. It was in such a situation that these countries became bankrupt. Later, one of the brains behind the cunning US economic manoeuvres of that time, John Perkins confessed to the world, shocking off-stage secrets in his book titled *Confessions of an Economic Hit Man.*

Seeing the pathetic plight of America today, waddling in the bog which America itself had created, it seems as if time is settling a score with it. Although it is a reality that America has become bankrupt, as long as dollar continues to be the reserve currency of the world, they would continue with the uncontrolled minting of dollars for market transactions. But if it loses its status as reserve currency, dollar would turn into a valueless note. Precisely because America is aware of this, it would prevent, at any cost, the attempts of countries to cut off ties with dollar. Similarly, monopoly companies in the US would also fight against such moves using any means.

It seems that America has abandoned the move to impose tax on US corporates that outsource jobs to other countries. Instead, it has decided to spread Cowboy Capitalism, with its ability to steal resources, into markets like India as well with the help of corporates in order to maintain the global superiority of dollar.

But the BRICS countries, in order to thwart this evil plan of the US, have reached an agreement as to use their own currencies instead of dollar in business transactions between themselves. For the past one year, China and Russia have been using their own currencies in transactions between themselves. Arab newspapers also hint that the GCC countries and Malaysia would also enter into such deals ('GCC and Malaysia Move Toward a Sustainable Economic Partnership', *Arab News*, 14 Novembers 2012). For quite some time, Malaysia too has been using their currency and the Chinese yuan for business needs. In the GCC Malaysia financial seminar held last October, Dr Abdullah bin Ibrahim, the financial expert from Saudi Arabia, opined that it would be preferable for the GCC countries as well to shift to this policy.

In any case, a massive problem the world would have to face in the coming days would be the currency war between America and China with currency value as their weapon.

4 December 2012

As the world's leading reserve currency,
US dollar was the central to the outbreak of currency war

15

THE CYBER WAR IN THE MIDDLE EAST

At the finale of this year, the world is observing that the Middle East, the stage for the first war in human history 5,500 years ago, has turned into a laboratory for a new war strategy. Through this new kind of warfare, the invisible enemy has targeted the relatively peaceful and economically strong nations in the region which has been the site of conflicts for centuries, owing to historical, political, and economic reasons. Though the cyber war does not lead to human causalities or bloodshed, it is more harmful than missiles or tanks.

It was on 15 August 2012 that the computer networks of Saudi Aramco, the world's biggest oil production company, came under cyber attack. Even though around 30,000 individual computers and some 2,000 servers were rendered dysfunctional in a matter of seconds and memory slots, where the data were stored, were damaged, fortunately, as Aramco's oil production control had not been linked to the internal communication system, it did not affect the processes that produced 10 billion barrels per day. Had it been otherwise, the consequences of the cyber attack would have been felt all over the globe. Experts in the field state that, in such a situation, the price of crude oil would have shot up from an average of 90 dollars to 200 dollars. It was on 9 December that Saudi Arabia officially revealed more details of the cyber attack against Saudi Aramco. The vice-president of Saudi Aramco, Abdullah Al Saadan, says that the main aim of the attackers had been to disrupt the flow of oil to the local and global markets. The spokesman of the Saudi Interior Ministry, Mansur Al—Turki, told the media that the hackers had executed the conspiracy from different countries in four continents. They had used the virus called the Shamoon for this purpose. One of the world's major producers of natural gas Qatar's RasGas also came under attack by the same virus, following the attack on Saudi Aramco. Industrial units in the Gulf countries are on the alert due to the threat of cyber warfare. The UAE government has formed an expert committee called the National e-Security to combat cyber attacks.

War in the twenty-first century has stretched beyond the realms of land, sea, and sky to the cyber world as well. By cyber world, it is meant Internet facility connecting computer networks across the world and the associated paraphernalia. The complex systems of computers, which are not connected directly by the Internet but are linked to each other like chain links, would also come under the realm of the cyber world. Attempting to infiltrate illegally into this system in order to dismantle it or seize control over it is called cyber warfare. If cyber criminals manage to seize control this way, they can extract information within the system and also manipulate effortlessly the associated functions, for example, transferring or withdrawing money from accounts, demolishing planes, sending missiles to wrong targets, and routing communication networks. Cyber spies can attack and exploit the service ports and transport systems operated by messages sent over computer networks, as well as the banking sector in a matter of seconds from secret locations. These virtual attacks from the cyber world cannot be kept at bay using warships or intercontinental missiles or by the power of the military.

Cyber criminals use Internet as the entry point for attacks. Their weapon is a software restricted to a few lines. The most dangerous missile in the cyber war is the Malware capable of destroying antivirus programmes installed to defend the system against dangerous virus software. It is estimated that each second, six new types of malware are produced in the cyber world. Like the ammunition industry, a massive industry linked to cyber crimes is flourishing in this new era. The responsibility of protecting a country's industrial units and the associated basic facilities from external attacks lies with the defence unit of the government of that particular country. But the biggest challenge for the cyber worlds of countries across the globe is the helplessness induced by the inability to protect them from cyber attacks from outside the country. Today, most countries have established cyber war units. But their virtual combating facilities do not form subject matter for public discussions. Precisely because the location of the enemy unleashing cyber attacks cannot be known, the totally one-sided cyber war has turned into a new threat to global peace.

Last June, The New York Times had reported American President Barack Obama's order to launch a cyber attack on Iran's atomic centre ('Obama Order Sped up Wave of Cyber Attacks against Iran', 1 June 2012). The report also says that it was the virus called Stuxnet born out of the US–Israel alliance that was used for the cyber attack against Iran's atomic power centre in 2010.

The cyber war plan, hatched by America against Iran during the presidency of Bush Jr had been baptised Olympic Games. America asserts that Iran is behind the cyber attacks using Shamoon virus against the energy-producing centres in Saudi Arabia and Qatar.

The mysteries of the new warfare being staged in the Middle East will be unravelled only if—along with scrutinising the politics of the armed conflict in Syria (which encompasses the world's first battlefield, Hamoukar), the reasons of Zionist terrorism in Gaza and the characters involved—the wars staged in the Middle East in recent years are subjected to re-examination.

31 December 2012

16

HIDDEN AGENDA TO GRAB THE MINERAL WEALTH

Are the US-European powers, in order to survive the period of economic depression when sources of income are drying up day by day, jeopardising the very existence of America and Europe, weaving the old colonial strategies once again? The intervention of France and America in Mali and Niger, respectively, strengthen the doubt as to whether Western Africa, rising up as the new Middle East, has become the venue for neocolonialism. As the imperialist strategies employed in Afghanistan and the Middle East, including Iraq, are being repeated in Africa, African countries are turning into the future preys of Western countries affected by the financial crisis. As to how the countries of Africa, referred to as the dark continent and the land of hunger till yesterday, would turn into the Middle East of tomorrow and a source of lucrative income for the West could be ascertained on a positive examination of the neo-imperialist strategies targeting the sub-Saharan countries.

Africa, with an area of 30 million square kilometres, is the second largest continent in the world. The fifty-four African countries are the seats of huge mineral wealth, including oil. It is estimated that 40 per cent of the world's gold deposits are in South Africa. Mali, where the French army intervened to rout the Al-Qaeda terrorists, stands third in gold production in Africa. It has also been found that Mali has uranium, diamond, and oil deposits. Thirty-one per cent of cobalt, uranium, bauxite, phosphate, and so on required for global needs are imported from African countries. Besides this, almost 57 per cent of chromium, diamond, and platinum reach other countries from Africa. The African country of Zambia stands second in the world in terms of copper production. Africa is a paradise of metals required for various electronic devices like flat-screen televisions, laptop batteries, and smart phones. Besides, 12.2 per cent of the world's total oil production belongs to Africa. It is said that, since African crude oil, like Saudi Arabian crude oil, has relatively less amount of sulphur, it is of high quality. Almost 25 per cent of the oil required for American's power requirements is imported from the African countries like Algeria, Angola, Gabon, Congo, and Kenya.

Of the world's ten countries which made financial progress in the last decade, six are African countries. As per the estimates of the World Bank, the sub-Saharan economic growth during this period was at a rate bypassing that of the Eastern countries including Japan. It was not for nothing the magazine *The Economist*, which had, years ago, written a cover story titled 'Hopeless Continent' about Africa ('Hopeless Continent', *The Economist*, 13 May 2000), corrected its stance and came out with a special edition on the progress of Africa ('Hopeful Continent', *Africa Rising*, 3 December 2011).

It is evident that the French army's arrival in Mali, its old colony, in January, under the guise of routing the Al-Qaeda terrorists, and America's deployment of the army, as well as pilotless drone planes for observatory flights in Mali's neighbouring African country, Niger, were all part of the secret agenda targeting Africa's natural resources. The American President Barack Obama's announcement to the world that the deployment of the army in Niger to root out Al-Qaeda on the same day (22 February) America stalled the resolution presented by Russia in the UN to condemn the bomb explosion executed by Al-Qaeda in Syria can be called an ironical imperialist joke. The Western media pretend to be blind to

America's policy of fighting against the Al-Qaeda in Mali while at the same time helping the latter in Syria.

It was one year back that the military captain Amadou Sanogo seized power by sabotaging the democratic government headed by Mali's President Amadou Toumani Toure, known as the guardian of democracy in Africa. It is said that Sanogo, who had attended military training in America seven times during the last eight years, had seized power in Mali with the benediction of the USA. France and America have linked hands in Mali under the guise of routing dissenters and their helper, the Al-Qaeda, for securing Captain Sanogo's government in order to protect their interests. It is sure that Mali and Niger, the countries of strategic importance to Africa, would become in the coming days permanent tenting grounds for imperialism on its African hunt. Earlier, Djibouti had been the sole American military station in Africa.

It should be realised that America's battle plans towards Africa are part of a pre-prepared plot. It was in 2007, during the tenure of George Bush Jr, that the military command called AFRICOM was formed to protect the US interests in African countries. The first war that AFRICOM fought in Africa was the Libyan War, which resulted in the assassination of Colonel Gaddafi. It was by using the Arab Spring as a screen that America thus brought to fulfilment its long-cherished desire to put an end to Gaddafi who had always been a hindrance to America's interests in Africa. It was on Christmas Day in 2012 that America revealed to the world its decision to deploy the US army under the responsibility of AFRICOM in thirty-five African countries other than Libya, including Sudan, Algeria, and Niger. The US diplomats knew very well that while the world was busy celebrating Christmas, the media would not take this issue up for discussion.

In this war for Africa's natural resources, Germany has also tented at Mali along with the neocolonialist imperialist faction with forces to deploy the army effectively. The head of the German Resource Alliance, Dierk Paskert, in an interview granted to Reuters on 18 February says that the German industries reliant on exports have been jeopardised owing to the unavailability of raw materials and that since natural resources like lithium, cobalt, chromium, and indium are becoming rarer, Germany should also be a part of the battle to ensure their availability even if it has to resort to force. German Resource Alliance is a group formed in 2010 by around twelve monopolised multinational German companies like Fox Wagon, Thyssen Bayer, and Bosch in order to ensure the availability of natural resources. It is the voice of the unholy alliance between imperialism, colonialism, and corporates in the offing to divide and appropriate natural resources that echoes in the words of Dierk Paskert.

China's wholesale import of rare minerals from Africa disturbs not just America but also European countries including Germany. Although the Chinese colonialism in Africa is sans war, it is rooted in highly exploitative market strategies. What China does in most of the African countries is sheer exploitation of the economic incapacity of these countries to mine their natural resources. China provides for the setting-up of basic facilities like transport and communication in these countries and, in turn, seizes the monopoly to drain away their natural resources.

It is sure that in the coming days, the world would see severe competition, remindful of the colonial era, between the major power centres for hegemony over natural resources. Along with this, in the race for the natural resources of Africa, the number of imperial-colonial alliances would also increase under the guise of combating terrorism as in the case of the Middle East.

11 March 2013

17

PEACE—A WEAPON IN THE MIDDLE EAST

The term *Middle East*, meaning West Asia or Near East, was coined by the English diplomats at the start of the twentieth century. It was a region in the middle of the financial and strategic important routes, linking their colonies in the farther east.

More often than not, the political tussles among the Middle East countries have led to severe losses to this region and profits to imperialist forces. As the conflicts in the Middle East turned into a threat to global peace, the imperialist forces reaped profits through weapon sales.

Three incidents, resulting from the progress in science and technology during the end of the twentieth century and the beginning of the twenty-first century, changed the political climate in the Middle East drastically. It was the Cassette Revolution fired by the speeches of Ayatollah Khomeini, who had been in exile in France during the Seventies when the use of tape recorders was widespread, that toppled the autocratic government of the Shah in Iran in 1979. Likewise, while analysing the changes that made themselves felt in this region in recent years, the glory of Al Jazeera, the Arab channel launched in 1996, cannot go unnoticed. Finally, the Arab Spring came into being in the Middle East, thanks to the freedom of expression opened up by technology in the form of Facebook and Twitter.

Post-Arab Spring, American foreign policy in the Middle East is not just failing but being pauperised. Uncle Sam does not have the sprite for another military adventure in this region. That is why the imperialist American forces and their main ally in the Middle East, Israel, are about to use peace instead of war as a weapon to deal with the changed sociopolitical realities. There is a goal of strategic importance behind this tactic. The rise of Iran as a major power in the Middle East is getting both America and Israel agitated. An Arab–Israel alliance against Iran is America's ultimate goal. As a first step towards this, the old motto of Israel–Palestine peace used now and then as per convenience is put forth now as a new promise.

Uncle Sam knows well that unless Israel announces its readiness to accept Palestine, the Arab world will not take Israel into confidence. This is precisely why both John Kerry, the US secretary of state, and Simon Perez, the president of Israel, argued unanimously for the recommencement of peace talks with Palestine at the World Financial Conference held at Jordan in May.

John Kerry, who had been in India on 23 and 25 June, left on 29 June to Israel for his fifth visit. He believes that the peace talks with Palestine can be resumed through his diplomatic manoeuvres. The Israel–Palestine peace talks had taken place last, five years back. They had come to a halt when Israel had embarked on a scheme of building houses at the West Bank, a Palestinian region which they had encroached upon.

The story of the attempts at peace made in Madrid under the auspices of America in 1991 was no different. Back then, America had tried to bring about a false peace between Israel and the Arab countries in order to make its intervention in the Middle East easier. If the current attempts are sincere, Israel should first convince the Palestinian people that the atrocities that had occurred sixty-five years back and that have been repeated afterwards would not recur.

The day the country called Israel took birth, 15 May 1948, is known as *yaumul nakba* ('day of catastrophe') in the Arab world. It was during this period that around 750,000 people were driven out from their motherland, Palestine. They were fated to flee with whatever they could grab hold of and spend their lives in refugee camps in the neighbouring countries. It was in order to concentrate the Jews scattered across the world at the centre of the Middle East, a region of strategic importance that another community was driven out.

The Nakba—when thousands, including infants, aged people, and women, were killed and atrocities inflicted, which cannot be confined to that particular era in history—kept on erupting relentlessly in Palestine.

Though history cannot be undone, it is a fact that the Palestine–Israel conflict cannot be resolved unless the rights of the Palestinians are recognised and they are given the freedom to live in their own land without fear.

The proposal put forth by Saudi Arabia in 2002 had been an excellent blueprint for peace. Arab countries would be willing to make up with Israel and engage in trade relations if the usurped regions are returned and Palestine is recognised as a sovereign nation with the borders of pre-1967 intact. The truth is that even when recognised thus, Palestine would get only 22 per cent of its land back.

Although the above-mentioned peace programme proposed by Custodian of the Two Holy Mosques King Abdullah bin Abdulaziz of Saudi Arabia at the Beirut Summit (2002) was read out over again at the Arab League Conference held at Riyadh in 2009, Israel has not agreed to accept it till now. This is precisely why one doubts the sincerity behind Simon Perez's rhetoric on peace.

Accepting Palestine does not mean that Israel would cease to exist. On the other hand, it is only when sincere efforts are on to correct the mistakes inflicted upon each other in the past and to prevent such mistakes from occurring again, then lasting peace would descend upon the central region of the Middle East. Other rhetorics would remain mere gimmicks with ulterior motives.

27 June 2013

Arab people fleeing from Palestinian villages in Galilee
as Israeli troops approach on 30 October 1948

Palestinian refugees making their way to Lebanon from Galilee in October 1948

Arabs leaving Haifa as Jewish forces enter the city, 21-22 April 1948

18

ARAB SPRING TURNING TO AN ARAB WINTER?

The Middle East is currently undergoing extraordinary developments. The bleeding squares of Egypt, worsening politics of Tunisia, and the internal strife in Syria are making the Middle East sleepless.

Two and a half years ago, when the Arab Spring gave the hope that it will lead the Middle East to a transitional stage, the world famous *The Time* magazine marked that historical period towards democracy by choosing the *protesting agitator* as its iconic person of the year 2011. The Tunisian Jasmine Revolution that initiated the Arab Spring and later the people's agitation that spread to Egypt, Yemen, and Libya weakened the autocratic governments, brought changes in the rule, and thus captivated the attention of the world. When it turned into a new paradigm of people's movement that embodied diverse voices, it was benchmarked as people's model for revolutions yet to come. It even inspired the Occupy Wall Street movement that formulated against excessive consumerism and corporate greed of the West.

However, after the military took over the rule of Egypt, sabotaging the Mursi regime, and blood was spilt on the squares of Egypt, including Tahrir, a new question is cropping up: Will the Arab Spring that bloomed in the Middle East give way to a withering winter?

The sixty-year history of Egypt (1952-2011), prior to Mohammed Mursi's ascension to power through an election, was the history of military rule under the three autocrats, namely Nasser, Sadat, and Mubarak. For the last two decades, the Egyptian economy has not been stable. When unprecedented rise in prices of food materials, inflation, corruption, and unemployment made people's lives unbearable and created anarchy in the society, people ousted the thirty-year-old Mubarak rule through agitation.

After the revolution, when Islamists came to power in Egypt through democratic process, the Americans naturally feared that it would hurt their political and economic interests in the Middle East. There is no doubt that America will sabotage even democratically elected governments of the Middle East if they do not comply with the wishes of USA; there are several instances to prove it. The support America gave to the military to sabotage the democratically elected Islamist government in Algeria in 1992, the military coup of 1997 in Turkey backed by America, and its unwillingness to accept the Hamas government in Gaza, which came to power in 2006, are examples from recent history.

Attempts are being made, helped by other imperial powers, to topple Erdogan's government in Turkey, which is now hailed as a model rule. Erdogan's decision to remove many of the military leaders from their respective positions suddenly on 3 August should be perceived in this backdrop.

The political strategy adopted by America was to back Mubarak's autocratic rule in Egypt while at the same time help the opponents of the rule covertly. When Mursi became the president, America did not change its stance in Egypt. One thing is clear: powers from within and outside the country had been scheming to oust Mursi right from the day he became the president. Information that the Egyptian military leadership has got help from imperial Zionist powers to topple the government is now coming to light.

Just two weeks earlier to the sabotage of the Mursi government, that survived barely 368 days, American Defence Secretary Chuck Hagel and a top military official Martin Dempsey had communicated with Egyptian military leaders, the CNN has reported. One has to read it along with the America's statement that the Egyptian military sabotaged the democratically elected Mursi government to save democracy in Egypt. What an irony!

Soon after the military overturned the Egyptian government, Israel's ambassador to Egypt congratulated the military chief Abdul-Fattah Al-Sisi and conveyed that he was not only a hero in Egypt but also an idol for all Israel's Jews, reported an Israel radio.

Egypt is the largest recipient of American military aid after Israel. Nearly 1.5 billion dollar was given to Egypt every year to protect America's imperialist interests and not for the Egyptians. Within weeks, America is going to handover four F16 fighter crafts to Egypt. America has continued this military support for many years to maintain its control over the Egyptian military and to keep the military leadership loyal to the interests of Israel and America. It is said that the military leaders took direct orders from Washington even during Mubarak's rule. Military officials were appointed as governors, village chiefs, and heads of public sector institutions during his rule. Military leaders who benefited from such special concessions did not wish to give up any of the privileges. However, the prevailing conditions of Egyptian administration made it easier for military chief Al Sisi to topple the Mursi government. Meanwhile, the decision to align with America without comprehending their hidden agenda and leaving Mubarak's foreign policy, as well as military organisations unchanged, led to Mursi's downfall.

Political observers are now apprehensive that slipping into a civil war, Egypt might give way to another Syria-like crisis in the Middle East. With the brotherhood in support of Mursi on one side and a section of people supporting the military for demanding Mursi's trial and the Tamarood movement taking to the streets on the other side, protests in many parts of Egypt are gaining momentum.

People's anger against the military rule is flaring up; it is difficult to predict where it will lead to. The political situation in Tunisia, where the Arab Spring started, is also not optimistic either. The assassination of the opposition leader Mohammed Al Brahimi in Tunisia a week ago has deteriorated the political situation. Opposition groups have grabbed this opportunity and are using pressure tactics on the government. The Tunisian Trade Union, a workers' movement, already has given an ultimatum to remove the democratically elected Prime Minister Al-Areed. However, Ennahda, the ruling party, has taken a firm stance against this. If outside forces do not interfere, it can be said that things are largely under the government's control in Tunisia even as protests for and against the administration are being staged.

But the future of the Arab Spring is not overcast by darkness. The rising protests against the military rule in Egypt are an indication to it. A severely cruel military attack on a rally of Mursi supporters led by the brotherhood was orchestrated last Wednesday. Under the circumstances that led to the loss of hundreds of innocent lives, Vice-President Mohammad Al Badari had to vacate his position. To know how hard the efforts will be, to triumph over the imperial agenda and reinstate democracy that has given hope to the Middle East, you may have to wait, but, surely, the wait will not be long!

21 August 2013

Hillary Clinton meets with Egyptian President Mohammed Morsi in July 2012

Tayyip Erdogan, Prime Minister of Turkey

IMAGE DETAILS

Images for Chapter 1

(1) **File name**—Chapter 1A (**Image Title:** Weapons ready for launch) link—http://commons.wikimedia.org/wiki/File:011031-N-3405L-007_Weapons_Ready_for_Launch.jpg

(2) Chapter1B (Plumes of smoke billow from the World Trade Centre towers in New York City after a Boeing 767 hits each tower during the 11 September attacks) link—http://en.wikinews.org/wiki/File:WTC_smoking_on_9-11.jpeg

Images for Chapter 2

(1) Chapter2A—Then US President George W. Bush delivers a speech, commemorating the sixtieth anniversary of the attack on Pearl Harbour to a group of Pearl Harbour survivors and sailors of the Atlantic Fleet on the flight deck aboard USS Enterprise) link—http://commons.wikimedia.org/wiki/File:011207-N-0063C-001_President_Bush_on_board_Enterprise.jpg

(2) Chapter2B (O. V. Vijayan) link—http://commons.wikimedia.org/wiki/File:O._V._Vijayan.jpg

Images for Chapter 3

(1) Chapter3A (George Orwell) link—http://commons.wikimedia.org/wiki/File:George_Orwell_press_photo.jpg
(2) Chapter 3 B (Nobert Weiner) link—http://en.wikipedia.org/wiki/File:Norbert_wiener.jpg

Image for Chapter 4

(1) Chapter4A (Iraq War protest poster) link—http://commons.wikimedia.org/wiki/File:Iraq_war_protest_poster.jpg

Images for Chapter 5

(1) Chapter5A (Saddam Hussein) link—http://commons.wikimedia.org/wiki/File: Iraq_Saddam_Hussein.jpg
(2) Chapter5B (Hugo Chávez during a tour of US Naval Ship) link—http://commons.wikimedia.org/wiki/File:Hugo_Ch%C3%A1vez_on_USS_Yorktown.jpg

Images for Chapter 6

(1) Chapter6A (Palestinian boys wearing Che Guevara T-shirts) link—http://commons.wikimedia.org/wiki/File:Palestinians_wearing_Che_Guevara_tshirts.jpg
(2) Chapter6B (Che Guevara visiting Gaza Strip during 1959) link—http://commons.wikimedia.org/wiki/File:Palestinians_wearing_Che_Guevara_tshirts.jpg

Images for Chapter 8

(1) Chapter8A (Barack Hussein Obama) link—http://commons.wikimedia.org/wiki/File:BarackObamaportrait.jpg
(2) Chapter8B (Mikhail Gorbachev) link—http://commons.wikimedia.org/wiki/File:Gorbachev_(cropped).jpg

Images for Chapter 10

(1) Chapter10A (Bernard Lewis) link—http://en.wikipedia.org/wiki/File:Lewis-pre.jpg

(2) Chapter10B (US President Barack Obama and Vice-President Joe Biden, along with members of the national security team, receive an update on Operation Neptune's Spear, a mission against Osama bin Laden, in one of the conference rooms of the White House Situation Room on 1 May 2011. They are watching live feed from drones operating over the bin Laden complex) link—http://en.wikinews.org/wiki/File:Obama_and_Biden_await_updates_on_bin_Laden.jpg

Image for Chapter 11

(1) Chapter 11A (Occupy Wall Street protesters at Zuccotti Park in Lower Manhattan near Wall Street) link—http://commons.wikimedia.org/wiki/File:Occupy_Wall_Street_(6352787834).jpg

Images for Chapter 13

(1) Chapter13A (Hosni Mubarak) link—http://en.wikinews.org/wiki/File:Hosni_Mubarak_ritratto.jpg

(2) Chapter13B (Tahrir Square during the 2011 Egyptian Revolution) link—http://commons.wikimedia.org/wiki/File:Tahrir_Square_on_July_29_2011.jpg

Image for Chapter 14

(1) Chapter14A (As the world's leading reserve currency, US dollar was the central to the outbreak of currency war) link – http://en.wikipedia.org/wiki/File:Hundred_dollar_bill_03.jpg

Images for Chapter 17

(1) Chapter17A (Arab people fleeing from Palestinian villages in Galilee as Israeli troops approach on 30 October 1948) link—http://commons.wikimedia.org/wiki/File:Flickr_-_Government_Press_Office_(GPO)_-_Arab_People_fleeing.jpg
(2) Chapter17B (Palestinian refugees making their way to Lebanon from Galilee in October 1948) link—http://commons.wikimedia.org/wiki/File:Palestinian_refugees_1948.jpg
(3) Chapter17C (Arabs leaving Haifa as Jewish forces enter the city, 21–22 April 1948) link—http://en.wikipedia.org/wiki/File:Haifa_Exodus_1.png

Images for Chapter 18

(1) Chapter18A (Hillary Clinton meets with Egyptian President Mohammed Morsi in July 2012) link—http://commons.wikimedia.org/wiki/File:Clinton-morsi.jpg
(2) Chapter18B (Tayyip Erdogan, prime minister of Turkey) link—http://commons.wikimedia.org/wiki/File:Recep_Tayyip_Erdogan.PNG